The Lost Countryside
Images of Rural Life

The Lost Countryside
Images of Rural Life

Chris Shepheard

Photographs from the archives of

The Herald
FARNHAM CASTLE NEWSPAPERS LIMITED

Rural Life Centre

breedon books
PUBLISHING

First published in Great Britain in 2001 by
The Breedon Books Publishing Company Limited
Breedon House, 3 The Parker Centre, Derby, DE21 4SZ.

ISBN 1 85983 260 1

Printed and bound by Butler & Tanner, Frome, Somerset
Jacket printing by GreenShires Ltd, Leicester

Contents

Introduction

The Lost Countryside? Surely it's always been like that. Such must be the response of many rural visitors and dwellers today. The countryside seems so timeless. Whatever change there is seems to happen very slowly and the overall picture remains much the same. Sure, the towns and cities have gradually expanded into the surrounding rural landscape, but there is still plenty of unspoilt country for all to enjoy.

In fact this idyllic vision is far removed from the truth.

When man first arrived in southern England the natural vegetation was dense deciduous woodland. In this, and close to water, he carved out clearings large enough for his small settlements and with enough land to support the community with food. Paths and tracks led through the forest to other nearby settlements.

One such settlement was probably established at or near today's village of Tilford in Surrey, the home of the Rural Life Centre. The museum of country life here records and preserves items from the surrounding area including an archive of photographs which form the core of the current volume.

Between man's arrival and the writing of this text, however, much change has occurred in the museum's collecting area, which includes the western half of Surrey, the eastern half of Hampshire, parts of West Sussex and even an area extending northwards into Berkshire.

Following the felling of trees to provide room for man's early attempts at agriculture, wood became highly prized as a source of fuel and building material. Much of the wood was turned into charcoal to fire early industries, including glass, iron and gunpowder. Timber from the forests still exists in some of our most famous buildings, notably the magnificent hammer-beam roof of Westminster Hall in London.

The wholesale industrial felling of trees caused an opening up of the landscape and created the heath and downland now so typical of large parts of the area. The clearance also allowed more agriculture to develop, not only to satisfy local needs, but also to feed the hungry mouths of rapidly growing London and other south-east cities and towns.

Improvements in cultivation methods and manuring brought increased yields, but only with the introduction of mechanisation could production begin to keep pace with demand. Jethro Tull's seed drill of around 1700 started this process, but man had already used animals to help with cultivation for many years. First oxen and then horses were used to draw single-furrow wooden ploughs through the soil, but soon machines were being used for many more processes.

At about the same time the Industrial Revolution and the ability to smelt iron using coal and coke meant the industrial heartland of Britain moved northwards. In turn better metal products meant that more complex machines for use on farms could be produced.

It is at about this point, in the 1860s, that photography began to become more widespread and popular. This single fact has allowed the production of this book, but also means that the illustrations only show the countryside from the second half of the 19th century onwards.

However, that century and a half has seen the most dramatic and rapid change of all in the British countryside. Farming and all other rural crafts and industries had always been extremely labour intensive, but machines meant that a reduced workforce could produce vastly increased yields.

The towns were growing apace, as manufacturing industries, fuelled by the Industrial Revolution, demanded more and more workers. Improving communications, both road and rail, meant it was easier for the country workforce to travel to the newly created jobs.

Agricultural machinery kept improving, making larger fields and even smaller workforces viable. For instance, where harvesting might have originally required two machines to produce the finished grain, along with numerous waggons to transport the crop back to the farmyard, the combine harvester completely automated the process in one operation.

At the same time, increasing prosperity and mobility meant that some town dwellers could move out to larger country properties to live, sometimes keeping their town houses as well. The urban workers, along with village residents, began to see the countryside in a new light – as a place to relax in their increasing spare time.

Soon there began to be spare capacity in the agricultural food production system, and not so much land was needed for agriculture. Gradually the countryside has begun to revert, at least in part, to how it must have looked when man first arrived here. This, of course, is of great benefit to the burgeoning tourist industry in the area, which today is the single most important factor in the rural economy.

At the same time villages are rapidly losing their traditional hearts. Most of the pubs and churches are still there, but shops and garages are fast disappearing, due largely to the lure of easily reached supermarkets designed around the car that nearly every family now owns.

Yet information technology means that office workers no longer need to travel to a central place of work. Their labours can be carried out from their country homes without any travelling involved at all. If this trend continues, village life could see a resurgence, with the settlements being populated during the working day instead of just during the evenings and at weekends.

Amazingly, we could be on the brink of a return to the original rural economy of small independent communities. They would lie scattered throughout this wonderful country landscape, providing a superb place to live and work, yet still connected to the wider world by modern technology.

If this were the case, there would be no fear of our countryside ever becoming 'lost' again.

Chris Shepheard
May 2001

Acknowledgements

The majority of the photographs and other illustrations in this volume have come from the archive at the Rural Life Centre, Tilford, and have been carefully selected and researched by members of the museum support group, the Rustics.

Readers of the *Herald* newspapers have, for many years, contributed their memories and photographs to the 'Peeps into the Past' column. This collection has provided much material. Former *Herald* chief reporter Monica Jones has enlivened the images with her memories of a childhood spent on a farm and working life as a rural reporter.

Maurice Hewins has acted as chief picture researcher, adding material from his own collection to those of the *Herald*, Geoff Lunn of the Sands, Mary Rapley and Norman Ratcliffe of the History of Thursley Society, Olivia Cotton and her Churt archives, plus many others, including Jim Tice, formerly of Runfold Farm, Sir Richard Thornton of Seale and Angus Stovold of Cross Farm, Shackleford.

Other museums have helped to fill gaps in the coverage and principal among these are the Museum of Farnham and the Museum of English Rural Life at Reading.

Geoff Lunn, a photographer in his own right, must be acknowledged for the large amount of work he has undertaken in the dark room working on images from numerous sources.

Finally, credit must be given to the many photographers without whose work this volume would never have seen the light of day. Many names are long forgotten, but those whose work is featured here include Jimmy Rawlings of Badshot Lea, John Henry Knight of Barfield, Runfold, Major Lane of Rowledge, several decades of staff photographers at the *Herald* and those that contributed to the ICI photographic archive.

Apologies to any one who has been missed out, and if readers can identify the sources of photographs, or add further details or images, the staff of the Rural Life Centre would be delighted to hear from you.

Chapter 1
Earning a Living

T HE COUNTRYSIDE is like the town in that, in order for the residents to survive, there has to be a way of 'keeping the wolf from the door'. Earning a living in the town has always been thought of as the soft option compared with those employed in the rural industries. This was certainly the case until the widespread introduction of mechanisation during the 20th century. Before this work usually involved intensive manual labour.

Traditionally, the main source of income for the area covered by this book was the woollen industry,

until it was superseded by hops in the 19th century. Shearers generally travelled from farm to farm offering their services under contract. Here a farmer looks on while his labourers carry out the preliminary task of washing the sheep. This ensured a cleaner fleece but was not the only time the sheep had to endure the indignity of a forced bath. Dipping of the sheep also took place about twice a year to rid them of parasites in their dense coats. Both operations were very labour intensive and led to the employment of much casual labour.

Unlike the other farmhands, the shepherd's life was often a lonely existence. He would spend much time alone with his flock, protecting them from predators and acting as midwife at lambing time. This Sussex shepherd is with his charges and faithful sheepdog on the South Downs, a lovely spot to be when the weather was good, although he needed protection from all the elements, hence his heavy waterproof coat and felt hat. Often the shepherd would live for months at a time in his portable hut on wheels, which was moved to the grazing lands by the farmer's horses. This would be equipped with a bed, chair and small wood-burning stove, the heat from which would protect the new-born lambs as much as the shepherd.

This shepherd seems much nearer to civilisation in his fold at Crondall, near Farnham. Usually made of wattle hurdling and thatched with straw, the fold protected new-born lambs like the one the shepherd is holding. At this time of the year, the dog's job was as much to drive off marauding predators like foxes and crows as to round up the sheep. He is resting beside the wooden hay rack, or crib, from which the sheep fed. If the ewe rejected her lambs, the shepherd also took on the task of bottle feeding.

Traditionally we visualise shepherds as the elder statesmen of the farming community. However, they all had to begin work earlier in life, and this young shepherd could well be standing in front of his first charges, proudly holding his first leg crook made by the local blacksmith. These are Downland sheep and, even on the chalk, the surface could be muddy, especially in the valley bottoms. This young man is sensibly attired, with leather gaiters attached to his working boots.

When grazing was in short supply, the sheep's diet had to be supplemented. This gang of labourers and their young companion have joined the shepherd to help slice up root vegetables with the mangold slicer. Some of the product can be seen on the ground, as yet untouched by the sheep behind. The temporary fencing to restrict the flock's movement across the mangold field is interesting. This is composed of twine netting and would have prevented the sheep from having access to the edible leaves of the whole field at once. Today's equivalent is the electric fencer and easily movable conductive netting.

This photograph from the *Herald* archives depicts a typical scene at lambing time and was taken somewhere in the Farnham area in 1950. Note the straw thatch on the top of the hurdles to give the ewes and lambs extra protection from keen winds and frosty nights.

As shearing time approached, the flock was brought down to the farm. Here itinerant shearers would assemble to remove the pre-washed fleeces. Mechanisation certainly eased the shearer's lot, first with hand-wound mechanical cutters with a boy usually providing the motive power, and later with portable engines or electricity driving the machinery.

Before this blacksmith-made shears had been the order of the day. They were kept extremely sharp and were often protected by a leather sheath when not in use. A good shearer was worth his weight in gold as he could work accurately, without injuring the reluctant animals, and fast. Any animals that did receive small nicks and cuts were treated with tar by the 'tarboy', to prevent infection entering the wound.

These shearers are working in a barn on Pierrepont Farm at Frensham, very near to the Rural Life Centre, probably at the turn of the 20th century. Sheep wait patiently beyond the doors while one of their number is clipped on the right. The shearer on the left has just removed a fleece, which he is winding in the traditional way, ready for it to be sent off to market packed into a woolsack.

The early years of the 20th century saw a sea change, with the introduction of mechanisation to the farm. These two views in Clifton's Field at Reigate in 1905 epitomise the change. The harvester with sickle and hook *(above)* is still employed to cut the standing crop around the edge of the field where the machinery cannot reach.

Meanwhile, three horses pull the reaper and binder through the majority of the wheat.

This is still a long way short of the modern combine harvester, but at least the corn is cut and bound into sheaves for the labourers to stook and keep dry until they are picked up and taken to the rick yard.

The harvested sheaves are stacked in ricks to await the arrival of the threshing gang. These contractors travelled around the farms with their machinery, which was beyond the means of the average farmer. In order to keep the grain dry, the crop was made into a rick on staddle stones, which also kept vermin away from the ears. The top of the rick was then thatched to keep out the inclement weather. It could be several months before the threshing drum had been to every farm and the grain could be on its way to the mill.

Of course the thatcher's main task was to weatherproof buildings. A good quality thatch, well laid, will last for 25 years or more, and even then only require replacement of the uppermost layers. This thatcher is at work at the Weald and Downland Open Air Museum at Singleton in West Sussex. The building is one of the many ancient buildings that

the museum has rescued from demolition and re-erected in the original form.

Thatching is one of those crafts that is once again in great demand. The problem now is getting enough long straw or reed suitable for the purpose.

Frank Polpolski and a colleague carry out the back-breaking task of harvesting potatoes by hand on Stovolds Cross Farm at Shackleford, near Godalming. This staple crop would be grown on the farm for supply to nearby towns and these men would probably go home to tend their own crop in the garden during their spare time.

Once picked, potatoes were often stored in a clamp at the edge of the growing field. The clamp was a long, low mound with the potatoes laid on straw and covered with more straw, and then the whole covered with soil to afford the crop protection from frost.

In the autumn the farmer would return, open the clamp and grade the tubers. This group around the potato riddle, or grader, are on Runfold Farm near Farnham in 1938. As the tubers passed through the riddle, they would fall through mesh at different points according to their size. The three sizes being separated here were 'chits', the smallest for animal feed, seed potatoes for next year's crop and 'ware' or eating potatoes.

Farmer Fred Tice is second from the left and also in the group are 'Lion' Cray, Alice Crumplin, Amy Sawkins and Nell Crumplin. Judging by the sacks, it was a good harvest.

Whatever the harvest, both sexes and all ages were often involved. This weatherbeaten group have just completed the potato harvest on a farm near Farnham, probably at around the end of World War One. These pickers may well have had the use of a mechanical lifter, but even this demanded a lot of bending. The pickers still had to bend to gather the tubers from the ground surface once they were exposed by the lifter.

Rural Recollections
by Monica Jones

IT'S TRUE that 'my' village, within three miles of a town on either side (and one an army town), was not strictly rural. But certainly before the war, and continuing into the 1970s, it was agricultural, with a dairy farm at its heart and farms and fields growing vegetables and hops on its doorsteps. Hop-kilns and the site of a moated manor were part of its fabric.

The village, bounded by four bridges on the approaches from the four points of the compass, was and still is a robust and independent community, rooted in its farming heritage. When incomers objected to the effluvium from the naturally manured fields, they were given scant sympathy by those who had known and often worked the fields since childhood. And when the sand and gravel barons made increasing incursions into the haymeadows and cornfields, public footpath rights were fiercely protected.

When I grew up there in the 1930s, many of the village people worked on the farm, men skilled in horse and dairy management, in hop cultivation and drying. Fields were ploughed, sown, hoed and harvested, mangolds dug, clamped and cut, hay ricked and corn threshed. Wives and daughters were employed picking the brussels sprouts and leeks on finger-freezing mornings.

Hop cultivation was a highly-skilled business. In much earlier years, the hops were grown on poles and in April these had to be sharpened and meticulously positioned. In May, as the vines started to grow, they were tied to the pole by women using rushes gathered and dried the previous summer.

But in my childhood, the hops were grown on three strings coming up from the ground in a fan shape. For us, it was better than any circus to watch the men walking on stilts to tie the strings which would support the hop bines to the horizontal wires 12 feet above. Later, stringing was done from a stage mounted on a trailer, drawn first by a horse and later by a tractor with a special narrow wheel gauge.

The women still had their skilled role, training the shoots clockwise round the strings – it was always considered that these shoots should reach the top of the string by 21 June, when the lower leaves would be stripped and the bines dusted and sprayed against pests.

Drying and bagging the hops in the kilns was even more skilled. The gang of six men slept in the kiln to keep the fires going day and night, to turn the hops and take them off the oasts at exactly the right moment, before they were pressed into 'pockets' by the hand-operated presses. It was always exciting to watch, and I envied those men when I went with my mother to take them home-made steak and kidney puddings and blackberry and apple pies for their dinner.

The stiltman, F.C. Smith, ties the coir strings to the top of the wire framework in Tice's hop gardens in Guildford Road, Farnham, during 1953. Meanwhile Mr T. Willis ties the strings off to the lower and middle wires. Each day Mr Smith could string an acre and a half of field using 15 miles of string.

We could buy nearly everything we needed in the village, and visits to the towns were rare. Next door to the farm was a bakery which had been run by the same family for decades. They were justly famed for their bread and buns and especially for traditional lardy cakes, made to their own special recipe, which were deliciously treacly and always attracted a queue when they were taken round the hop gardens at picking time. When my father was a little boy, a bag of hot cross buns was regularly pushed under the hedge for his April birthday.

The bread was cooked by the old-fashioned bavin (wood-fired) method. Branches and twigs of trees, preferably oak, were cut and bundled together to make bavins and these were pushed into the oven and lit to heat the brick lining. The ashes were then drawn out and water sprinkled in to create steam and lay the dust and the trays of dough put in to cook; result, a lovely crust loaf.

Sometimes, Christmas geese and turkeys were cooked for the village in the bakery oven, and I remember this happening during the early war years, to save fuel.

There was another family bakery in the village, and one member of the family, Charlie, sang in the church choir for over 80 years, and for almost as long was regularly seen cycling round the village. He epitomized a village determined to do its own thing in its own unique way.

Hop pickers of all ages pose for the camera at Runfold Farm.

After the completion of the season's picking the carter collects up the pickers' willow baskets ready for another year.

Alongside the more common and well-known crops grown in Surrey were plants used in the production of essential oils. These included lavender and peppermint, among others, and there was a liquorice factory at Woking. Here workers pick a mint crop using small sickles before pitchforking it onto the waiting cart, probably during the 1950s.

These two agricultural workers could easily be confused with the mint pickers above, although they are obviously dressed for more inclement weather. However, Marie Andrews and Daphne March were actually forestry workers when photographed in 1957 at the Tilhill nursery in Tilford. Note the young seedling trees around their feet.

Showing the other end of a tree's life, this photograph depicts a hand-felling gang who have just toppled a mighty oak. Their large axes would have been used to make a felling notch, which determined the direction of fall of the tree. Then it would be down to just two men and the double-handed saw that can be seen curving down from the butt of the felled trunk. Despite the flexibility of the saw blade this must have been back breaking work, and the introduction of the petrol-powered chain saw eased the foresters' lot enormously.

Once the timber was felled it had to be turned into usable material for a wide range of purposes. Here Richard Pharo's traction engine is seen powering a portable saw bench mounted atop an old cart. This could be taken around from site to site as necessary. The photograph was probably taken in the Farnham area, as Pharo's were based in Badshot Lea, a village about three miles from the town centre.

The natural vegetation of all of this part of southern England was woodland. It provided the fuel for some of the country's earliest industries: iron, glass and gunpowder to name but three. Generally the trees were cut down and turned into charcoal by itinerant burners who went from wood to wood.

After cutting the woodland was allowed to coppice, and the younger, smaller resulting trees spawned a whole new series of timber-based crafts. Here a woodsman is seen cutting a chestnut coppice and trimming up the timber near Midhurst. The wood could be used in any number of ways, some shown in the other photographs on the next few pages.

This gate hurdle maker was photographed in his woodland workshop by Farnham farmer, inventor and early photographer John Henry Knight, during the 1880s. Note the stack of finished work behind the woodsman's shelter, and the side axe with which he performed most of his work.

The other common sort of hurdle was the wattle hurdle, which was used in the shepherds' folds. These too were made in the coppice, and this craftsman is thought to be working close to Elstead, again in the 1880s. Here the wood used is younger and thinner. It is riven, often with a sharp hook, and then each half is woven around uprights set in a wooden block on the ground. When completed, the panel can be removed and is held together purely with the tension of the weave.

Similar weaving was performed by the hedger and a well-laid hedge is totally stock proof. Here a farmer examines a newly-laid hedgerow at Wyard's Farm, Alton, in 1959. The uprights of the existing hedge are partly cut through and woven through the adjacent stems. Occasionally, as here, additional uprights are driven in for support. The partly-cut stems continue to grow and the wound soon heals, making a hedge with uniformly thick vegetation from top to bottom.

Two Farnham council workers use a cross-cut saw to cut up a dead willow tree alongside the River Wey in the town's Gostrey Meadow. Such trees were regularly pollarded, originally to provide the small young shoots required by local basket weavers, but later to keep the trees to a manageable size and prevent limbs and whole trees from falling into the watercourse, where the potential for flooding has always been high.

Carter George Prince arrives at Greatham Manor Farm with a load of bavins, probably bound for the farm's bread oven, in around 1900. Such ovens were heated by burning bavins, or bunches of small twigs, and the ash inside was cleared out before the freshly moulded dough was introduced.

The waggon (note the spelling, peculiar to this area of Britain) George sits upon was made by Smiths of Basingstoke and is typical of the Hampshire pattern. Every county had its own, slightly different design, and its own colour scheme too.

Frensham Ponds, just south of Farnham, has long been a popular spot with visitors, particularly on sunny weekends. Large numbers would drive down from London and crowd the sandy beaches. The ponds were originally created to provide a supply of fresh fish for the Bishop of Winchester, who lived in Farnham Castle.

Today the only boats allowed on the water of the Great Pond are from the sailing club, which holds competitive events there most weekends during the summer. Here we see the weed cutter in use in 1951, used to ensure the dinghies had a smooth and uninterrupted passage.

All the working photographs so far have shown outdoor occupations. Here, however, the lady seamstresses of Churt are busy making costumes for the entertainers of Murray's Nightclub during the 1950s. In charge is Elsie Burchmore, who is checking details on a nearly finished garment.

The seasonal nature of farming has always meant a wide fluctuation in the need for labour. Today this is made less noticeable by the heavy use of mechanisation, but still whole families come to the Surrey and Hampshire border area for a working holiday at the end of August to help with the hop picking.

In the village of Bentley there is still a row of prefabricated hop pickers' barracks in annual use, probably the last surviving buildings of this type. However, this family, pictured in the village in 1959, brought their own caravan. Others behind are making use of an old bell tent for their 'holiday accommodation'.

Three years earlier than the previous view, these two families are probably homeward bound, on the Crondall road out of Farnham. They are still using horse-drawn caravans in the traditional style, and are passing the the road to Wimble Hill Isolation Hospital. The town of Farnham can just be made out in the valley, as the horses pull their heavy loads up the hill from Dippenhall.

Hop picking was the main occupation for travellers in this area each year, but what did they do the rest of the time? Another Mecca for these families was Epsom Downs, for the Derby. Here they entertained the vast crowds of Londoners that thronged there for their 'day out in the country'. This photograph of a family of buskers probably dates from the early 1900s.

Chapter 2

Home Life

PHOTOGRAPHS of country homes always seem to show an idyllic scene. This view of Smallbrook Farm at Thursley was taken in around 1883 and is no exception. However, the exterior appearance often belies the hard times experienced by the residents.

Life was far from easy in the countryside. Income often depended on the vagaries of the weather; agricultural labourers' wages varied with the amount of work they were able to do. To help ease the family over the hard times, all members were required to work in some capacity whenever possible. This could vary from taking in washing to stone picking on farmers' fields.

The Levy family pictured here, including Eliza-

beth, Lizzie, Maria, Ann and William, had probably experienced varied fortunes despite living in this splendid farmhouse.

Today Thursley village is unspoiled by modern development, although it also no longer supports any businesses and very few of the residents work in or around the village. The houses, such as Smallbrook Farm, fetch high prices, which are beyond the means of local youngsters.

So the village homes which for so long were the centre of family life, where all members would return after a hard day's local labour, are now little more than bedrooms for city and town workers during the week. Weekends are the only time that any semblance of the old village lifestyle returns.

Another Thursley family pose proudly in front of their home at Highfield Farm in around 1900. E. Baker took on this farm in 1879 and it stayed in the same family until 1945 when John Baker retired. There are at least three generations of Bakers in this photograph. Note that the senior member of the family carries a tool, almost as a symbol of his craft. Unfortunately the head of what could be anything from a garden rake to a shepherd's crook is missing from the photograph.

Tyrone Cottage at Compton just outside Guildford. At the time, in 1919, it was owned by R. Stovold, who is probably the gentleman standing proudly outside his home. Often a countryman's home was also his place of work, with his trade carried on in outbuildings to the main house. This seems to be the case here. Mr Stovold wears a farrier's leather apron, split up the centre to accommodate the horse's leg, while the craftsman attaches the shoe. Other clues to the occupation of the man are the sledge hammer carried over his shoulder, the lengths of iron and steel bar propped up against the tree and building and the wrought iron 'curls' hanging on the right hand tree.

A young Ian Gotelee gets a breath of fresh air while out in his pram in Runfold, near Farnham, accompanied by his nanny and grandmother, Ada Tice. Alongside walk two Land Army farm workers including Muriel Middleton on the extreme right, who also later became a Tice when she married the farmer.

Rural Recollections
by Monica Jones

WE HAD electricity in the farmhouse before the war, although I remember when there was only gaslight. The white globe-shaped gas mantles were as fragile as the blown birds' eggs collected by my father when he was a boy and which I so satisfyingly crushed one afternoon at the age of three.

We had a gas cooker, although much of the cooking was done by the black-leaded kitchen range. But the farm cottages had no electricity, gas or hot water until the 1950s when a modernisation programme was undertaken.

We saw little of our father and rarely ate together as a family except at Sunday roast-dinner time. We took it in turns to have Sunday tea with our parents in the drawing room, with raspberry jam-sandwiched Victoria sponges and seed cake. A bedtime favourite was bread (cut into cubes) and milk with golden syrup poured over. The milk was brought across from the dairy in an open tin can, often with a wisp or two of hay floating in it. It had been cooled but not pasteurised - we didn't seem to

worry much about germs then, although we were dosed with brimstone (sulphur) and treacle in the spring 'to purify the blood'.

Whooping cough and measles were rife and we suffered from both; going out into the hop gardens was supposed to be good for the former (or a visit to the gasworks). And I remember when we were recovering from chicken pox, we had to climb out of the bedroom window onto a ladder to reach the garden, so as not to spread the germs through the house.

Our food was mainly home-grown, the Best of British and strictly seasonal, except perhaps runner beans, which were usually so prolific that they were eaten with a marked lack of enthusiasm when they were old and stringy and were salted down for the winter.

For instance, we ate rhubarb endlessly in the early spring; later the vast spreading leaves made splendid play umbrellas for us children. In the early summer it was all gooseberries - gooseberry fool, gooseberry pudding, gooseberry tart - and strawberries at my grandmother's croquet parties.

New green peas were another delectable, warmly-anticipated treat. We were often sent to pick them and once, when joined by friends, came back with a mere score of pods; the rest lay empty among the pea sticks, the sweetness of their uncooked contents proving irresistible; our mother was not amused.

Other seasonal foods were fresh field mushrooms, Michaelmas goose in September (the geese got a bit fat by Christmas), greengages and damsons ripe from the tree, blackberries of course and whortleberries ('hurts' to us) picked from the bushes that covered Crooksbury hill.

There was boiled leg of mutton (we had mutton then, not lamb – and boiling fowl) served with caper sauce, hare jugged with port wine and rabbit cooked with lots of herbs and onion with a crust of browned breadcrumbs. And liver with 'crow' – the crunchy, tasty fat it came with.

The Sunday chicken (we took turns to have the parson's nose) was preceded by a luscious steamed dripping pudding, over which the fat from the roasting pan was poured and on which, as on Yorkshire pudding, appetites were blunted before the main course.

Puddings, especially suet puddings, were a constant dietary factor; not only rhubarb and apple, but also spotted dick, jam roly-poly and treacle, all served with gallons of custard. And of course in July there was summer pudding with its filling of blackcurrants, redcurrants and raspberries.

In the seemingly spacious stone-floored wood-shelved larder, down two steps, were the earthen-

Edie and Nell Crumplin pose outside their Badshot Lea cottage home in 1911. The house stood in what is now Rankine Close but has since been demolished. It had been built by a squatter on the parish waste and, even by the standards of the day, was a poor little dwelling.

Daniel Rampton and his daughter Mabel stand at the gate to Broadhatch Cottage, Bentley, in around 1910. Daniel was a former shepherd to J. Alfred Eggar's family, who farmed in the Bentley area, just east of Alton.

In those days, single daughters were expected to look after a bereaved parent. In contrast to the last photograph, this cottage still stands and is a highly priced country residence.

ware crocks of the salted runner beans and eggs in isinglass, preserved for the winter. On the shelves were ranged the home-made chutneys, pickled onions and jam, and the rubber-ringed Kilner jars of plums and greengages. We had no fridge of course, and dishes of left-over cold meat and pies (though we were always exhorted by my father to 'eat everything up') stood on marble slabs under

Another picturesque country home in the Thursley area, this time in the bottom of the Devil's Punchbowl near Hindhead. This is Keeper's Cottage, seen during the early 1900s with a well-tended vegetable garden and a couple of chickens scrabbling in the dirt.

At the time the owner probably worked as a broomsquire, making besom brooms from the heather that thrives on the nearby common. He was the subject of a novel of the same name written by Sabine Baring-Gould, which deals with the horrific murder of a sailor on the nearby Portsmouth road, whose body was found by the broomsquire.

Later the cottage became the home of the National Trust warden for the area, so much of which is in the organisation's care.

Still in Thursley, Maria Baker gets out and about with the aid of her granddaughter and a wicker bath chair. These are the Bakers of Highfield Farm, shown in an earlier photograph. The family's dogs seem delighted with the outing too, but are paying no attention to one of the farm's cattle in the field. The country air obviously agreed with Maria, and when she passed away in 1941 she was the grand age of 91.

their bead-fringed net covers, immune to the flies which were fascinatingly caught on the sticky overhead fly papers.

In the stone-floored scullery were the copper used for boiling the sheets and the mangle; once butter was churned there, and I did not like that tedious, handle-turning job.

I think smells are the most evocative of all the senses: the smell of the steam from the Monday wash, the singeing over the gas stove of the chickens which had just been plucked, the pungency of dung-heaps, horse sweat and milk-mouthed calves. Above all (for me) the rich, mealy, fundamental smell of the corn store, stirring all the senses.

Elizabeth Levy *(left)* and her sister Mrs Wood tend the garden at Hedge Cottage where they lived. This is part of the Smallbrook Farm estate at Thursley. Elizabeth was born in 1823 and survived into the 20th century, dying in 1912 during her 89th year.

My mother had help in the house and with us children, but we had to help with the chores, like topping and tailing gooseberries and podding peas.

The greatest set-to was the annual spring-clean, an obligatory, drastic and traumatic ritual. All the winter curtains came down, the paintwork and all the crockery and ornaments were washed and the carpets were taken up, hung over the washing line and beaten.

This was our job; enthusiastically at first, and then with flagging arms and spirits, we wielded our discarded broken-stringed tennis racquets as the clouds of dust rose about us and the burgeoning garden, fields and woods beckoned us to less laborious springtime delights.

Another view at Smallbrook Farm shows Maria Levy tending the chickens. Poultry was a useful supplement to a family's income and provided a ready supply of eggs for baking and fresh meat at the end of their laying lives.

Besides chicken, if there was sufficient space, a farm would often keep a flock of ducks on a pond usually close to the farmhouse to afford some protection from marauding foxes. Here the farmer's wife checks on her animals at East End Farm in Puttenham Road at Seale. Careful inspection reveals that there are chickens among the ducks. Almost hidden behind the lady is the very well behaved farm dog sitting in front of his kennel, an effective deterrent against the prowling foxes.

Another way of raising a little extra income, especially once cycling and the motor car became popular ways for town and city dwellers to visit the countryside, was to open your home as a tea shop. This 1920s photograph shows Crane's tea shop in Churt, between Farnham and Haslemere. Two of the staff are looking over the hedge in the hope of attracting some passing trade. From the sign it would appear that this family also provided a bakery and confectionery business for the villagers.

Interior views of country homes are rare, mainly due to the lack of light and the insensitive nature of the films then in use. Most that do exist show carefully posed scenes such as this, and are often taken in the home of the amateur photographer himself. Photography was not a pastime for the poor so most views are of the more well-to-do households. Here two young ladies are busy carding and spinning wool in front of a rather ornate, almost arts and crafts movement, fireplace. Probably for them such work was just a pastime, but in many cottage homes it brought in cash which made country living just that little bit more bearable.

In some areas, notably around Godalming, spinning, weaving and knitting was a large-scale cottage industry supplying garments to the numerous businesses in the town, whose products were known far and wide.

Still surviving today, and in a very similar setting with no encroaching development, this cottage in Thursley sits alongside the parish church and was once the vicarage. Apart from the now made-up road little has changed, principally because this road, The Street, is a dead end that leads up on to the common and attracts little traffic.

A typical village street scene in Boundstone Road at Rowledge. Now there are more houses between the cottages shown and the vegetation has grown to maturity, with sizeable trees flanking the road. In the distance a few cars can be made out. Today there are many more and it would be a very foolhardy subject who would pose for the photographer as nonchalantly as this gentleman. The interesting chimney stack has gone too, and the purpose of building it with the kink has never been explained.

Badshot Lea was a more developed village, with buildings grouped much more closely. On the left is a flint cottage in Badshot Lea Road. The house is still there but the adjoining hop kiln has been demolished now with the disappearance of hop growing from the village. Before demolition, however, it was also used as a boys' club established by John Henry Knight and for band practice. This might have been welcomed as a mixed blessing by the occupant of the 'big house' opposite behind the brick wall. Peckham-Williams, a noted hop grower, lived in Badshot Place here. Now a large housing estate occupies the site, grouped around the restored village pond.

A Frensham family dress up in their best clothes for a portrait by the local photographer. Mr Sturt, the local postmaster, commissioned a large number of photographs of the village and its surroundings. Many of the original glass plate negatives were found in the cellar of the old post office a few years ago and are now in the hands of the local history society. This archive provides a very good record of life during the early years of the 20th century.

A well-tended garden was every village householder's pride and joy. It provided a place to relax with the family in the summer, as well as supplying much needed nourishment in the form of home-grown vegetables. However it was still good to go out for the day and for many families a picnic in the nearby countryside was as far as they got.

Mr Langridge kept the Cricketers public house in Badshot Lea. Here the family take to the fields for a break from their home and work which shared the same premises. Again they are all dressed in their finest clothes for this special occasion.

Another large family group in the garden, this time for a very special occasion. Unfortunately we know few details, but this is a wedding group assembled in the vegetable patch of a Farnham garden, probably during the 1910s or 1920s. The bridegroom appears to be a sailor. At this time photography was still a slow and laborious process and the effort of standing still proved too much for some of the younger members in the

group, including one of the bridesmaids. Blinking was also a problem, as it still occasionally is, and the photographer has had to carry out some retouching work to the eyes of the bride's mother.

Two different views of the same road junction in Weybourne, taken by John Henry Knight in around 1900, show a typical village centre in this area. By this time the main crop was hops and the poles can be seen in the field beyond the large elm tree.

This predates the use of a wire framework used for cultivation shown earlier. Here the hop plants just grew up single poles, which were lifted from the ground so the pickers could strip the bines at harvest time.

The tree gave its name to the public house which stood behind and to the right of the photographer's position. The next pub, the Running Stream, is also visible beyond the tree. Agricultural labour was thirsty work and the area is renowned for the number of inns it supported.

The bungalow still stands at the crossroads but the elm tree has long gone, having been removed in a road-widening scheme, and a row of council houses stands in the hop garden. The washing on the left belonged to the Pearl family, who once lived at this now very busy and virtually unrecognisable junction.

Chapter 3
Village Trades

TODAY most villages in our study area consist of little more than houses around a church. During weekdays little happens as everyone is away working in towns and cities. Life only returns in the evenings and at weekends. In the past, though, each village was a thriving community in its own right. People lived here and worked here, either in the village itself or on surrounding farms.

Every village had its pub and shop, and many had other businesses besides. Commonest of these was probably the village blacksmith, like the one shown here, usually situated in the centre of the community, often beside the village green. He was responsible for all farm repairs as well as making many items from scratch, often recycling old metal parts from his scrap heap, a regular feature of the village smithy.

Often his premises adjoined, as here, or were even incorporated with the wheelwright's. The two went hand in hand as the smith produced all the metal parts needed for the construction of waggons and carts.

FIRST DAY'S SALE.

ISINGTON, BINSTED,
HANTS.

To WHEELWRIGHTS, BLACKSMITHS & OTHERS.
SALE OF STOCK-IN-TRADE.

Mr. J. ALFRED EGGAR

Has received instructions from the Executors of Mr. W. Smith, to Sell by
Auction, on the premises, at Isington,

On SATURDAY, FEB. 25th, 1888,

At 12 o'clock precisely, a quantity of useful

Furniture and the Stock-in-Trade of the Grocer's Shop,

AND

On MONDAY, FEB. 27th,

At 12 o'clock, the valuable STOCK-IN-TRADE of a

Wheelwright & Blacksmith

Comprising a large quantity of well-seasoned

Oak, Ash, Elm and Deal Plank Boards, Flitches, Scantlings, &c.,

About 1000 Oak Spokes, 700 well-seasoned Felloes,

Waggon Stocks, Axles, Arris Rails and Ladders.

OAK, ASH AND ELM TREES,

And a large quantity of Tools. The contents of the Blacksmith's Shop include
three pairs of nearly new Bellows, Anvils, Vice, Water Troughs, Tire-Bending
and Drilling Machines, Tiring Platform, Screw Tackle, Hand Drill, Band Saw
(nearly new), a large quantity of

BAR, SHEET, ROD AND HOOP IRON.

*Chains, Horse Shoes, Nails, Screws, Bolts, Pins, Butts, Spades, Shovels, Rakes,
Drug Bats and Tanks, the contents of the Painters' Shop,*

TWO RICKS OF HAY AND STUMP OF DITTO,

Also a useful Pony, Spring Cart and Harness.

*Catalogues on the Premises, at the Inns in the Neighbourhood, and of the
Auctioneer, Farnham, Surrey.*

Printed at the " Surrey and Hants News " Office, 1, Borough, Farnham.

This sale bill of 1888 deals with the contents of a typical wheelwright's and blacksmith's workshop at Isington, a small hamlet close to Bentley, midway between Alton and Farnham. Felloes (pronounced 'fellies') are the sections of the wheel's rim and the hoop iron would have been used to make the iron tyres, which would have been attached to the finished wheel on the tiring platform.

In larger villages the blacksmith would have quite a large staff, as here at Liphook. This village straddled the main London to Portsmouth road and would have seen much horse-drawn traffic, creating a thriving shoeing business for the farriers based here.

The man third from the left in this photograph holds a large die used for cutting screw threads and leaning against the anvil is a pickaxe head made by the craftsmen.

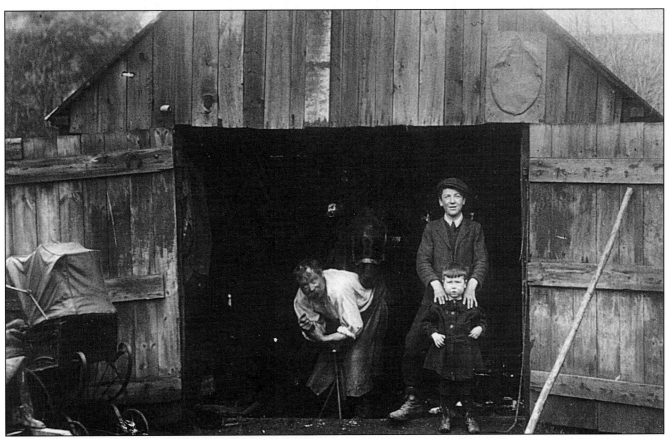

An altogether smaller smithy, this time at Churt. The building is just a wooden hut, but what goes on within is enough to attract the boys of the district from a very early age. Mr Karn, the smith, is busy shoeing a horse, watched by his young audience. Is the pram on the left another spectator or has it come in for repair?

Two farriers at work at opposite ends of Surrey. Above is Mr Bovington, the Elstead blacksmith, at work in his smithy on the small green in the village during 1952. He is rasping the hoof to ensure it fits snugly to the shoe. The smithy building still exists but has been completely rebuilt to house a very up-market office.

On the right is a farrier in Ewell removing the old nails from the horse's hoof before fitting a new shoe. He is wearing the traditional and practical farrier's split leather apron.

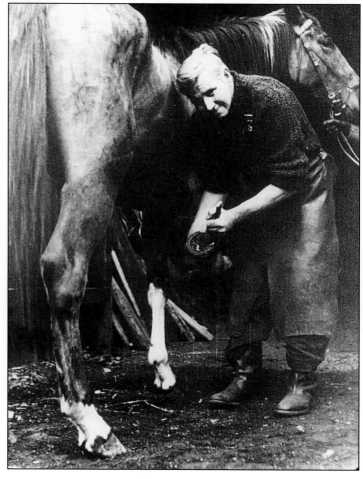

The staff of Sturt & Goacher, the famous Farnham wheelwrights, pose for the camera with examples of their work. The top photograph shows the men with some of the wheels they have made, and several of them are holding tools such as hammers, spokeshaves and axes. Below they stand in St Cross Road, with the workshop to the right and a fine range of their carts parked on the left.

George Sturt, that famous chronicler of local country living during the second half of the 19th century, was born into the wheelwright's business run by his father. His Hampshire and Surrey waggons are now prized items and the Rural Life Centre is fortunate to have one in its collection.

When cars began to appear on the roads, the firm went over to producing wooden bodies to fit on bought-in chassis. The workshop is still in existence, though it has been extensively rebuilt, and today houses part of a showroom for luxury cars.

The wheelwrights of Hillgrove in Sussex pose outside their workshop, above with a partially completed carriage wheel and below during the tiring process on a waggon wheel. The carriage wheel has the spokes fitted into the nave (or hub) but is awaiting fitting of the felloes. Beside the men are carts and waggons in various stages of construction and repair.

Once the wooden wheel was assembled it would have been fitted to the tiring platform. The iron tyre would then be heated on a fire and fitted to the wheel. The tyre would be made to be a very tight fit on the wood so that when it was cooled by water being thrown over it, it would shrink, thus tightening the spokes, felloes and hub. In Sussex, where the roads were heavy clay, the waggon wheels were very broad. Instead of tyres these were fitted with strakes, as shown below. These too were heated before fitting, so the workmen are using tongs, then nailed so as to cover the joint between two felloes. While this was happening the felloes were held in place by a tool called a samson. The wheel was partially suspended in a pit filled with water, and once the strake was fitted the wheel would be rotated to quench the heat and shrink the metal to fit snugly.

This wheelwright, Mr Instone, is fitting a new wheel onto the tiring platform before attaching a new tyre. This platform is quite a sophisticated model at Cove, near Farnborough in Hampshire. Below the platform is a tank full of water. By pulling on the lever leaning on the fence, once the hot tyre is fitted, the platform can be made to rotate and descend into the water to quench the tyre. More normally water would have to be thrown over the wheel rapidly and evenly to avoid splitting the wooden felloes or spokes.

This wheelwright is working 'in the field' during the 1920s, probably repairing the shafts on a timber carriage. The vehicle would be used to bring trees from the wood where they were felled to the rack sawbench visible in the background, powered by the steam traction engine. Notice the plane and spokeshaves in the foreground, along with the craftsman's tool bag.

Many villages in this part of the country had their own brickworks, as there was abundant suitable clay in the area. Today the flooded clay pits often provide attractive woodland features. Above, the staff of Hammer brickworks near Haslemere pose with the company's steam lorry in front of a kiln being built. The 'green' unfired bricks were stacked in clamps like this and then the fuel, packed throughout the stack, was ignited. The outer layers of bricks, which would be poorly fired, would have been used again and again in the same position.

The different firing temperatures created by this method led to the wide variety of brick colours which make local houses so attractive. Large developments often merited the construction of their own temporary brickworks and this was also the case with country estates.

Other brickworks, like the one at Crondall where the man *(right)* is working in 1955, also produced tiles. He is batting a hip ridge tile over a wooden mould. Today the site of Crondall brickworks is itself a small housing development, with the old pit filled in and levelled.

Another brickworks close to Haslemere, but this time the process shown is pugging, or mixing the clay. Once dug the clay was left to weather for some months before being put into this simple machine. The drum contained knives set into the centre spindle, which cut and kneaded the clay as the horse walked around the circle.

The clay would then go to the throwers, who literally threw the clay into the wooden moulds, forcing it into every corner.

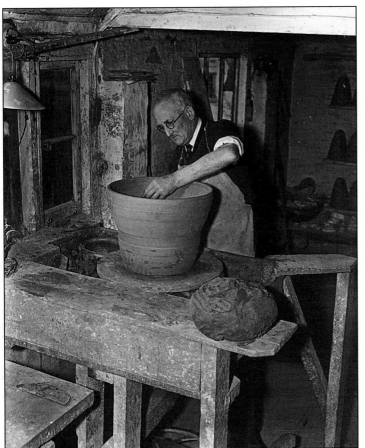

Wrecclesham Pottery was another user of the local clay. The pottery industry in this area can be traced back to Roman times, when up to 70 kilns operated in nearby Alice Holt Forest. This pottery was renowned for its terracotta wares and also its vivid green and blue glazes. The business was started at Elstead by Absalom Harris in 1860 and moved to converted farm buildings in Wrecclesham in 1873. The Harris family only relinquished the business at the very end of the 20th century.

Fortunately the buildings have been bought by a preservation trust who hope to re-establish pottery workshops here, so that scenes like these will once again become part of the village's daily life.

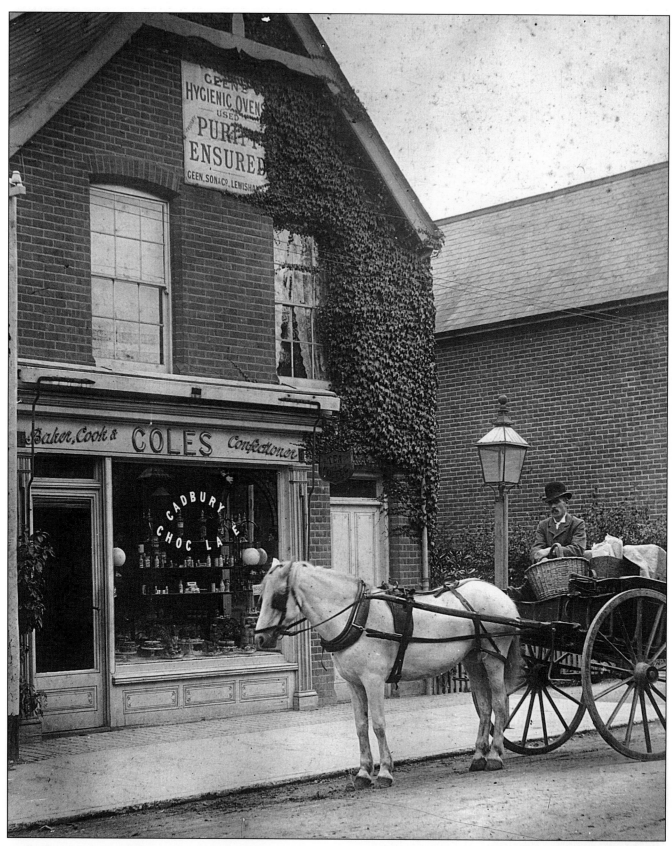

Small villages would have had just one shop which supplied most of the daily needs of the villagers. A trip into town for shopping was a rare occurrence for most country dwellers.

Larger villages would have had specialist shops like this bakers in Fleet, complete with delivery trap parked outside. This would have delivered to outlying settlements. The business subsequently became Allens before closing down in the 1980s. It is no longer a bakers but fortunately many of the fittings were saved and brought to the Rural Life Centre to form part of the museum's bakery display.

Selborne, between Alton and Petersfield, had only a few shops, so Maxwell's, which is shown here, dealt in a wide range of goods from furniture to groceries. Today there is just one grocer's shop in this popular tourist village and Maxwell's is now a gallery displaying and selling the works of disabled artists.

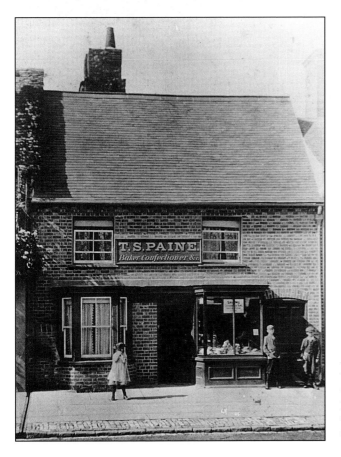

Another Fleet baker's shop attracts children, probably hoping for a sample or two. This is an altogether smaller shop with the proprietor's living rooms also on the ground floor alongside. The building shows interesting brick patterning produced by the builder sorting through the bricks as he laid them and using the different colours produced by the different firing temperatures mentioned earlier.

An unusual photograph of a shop interior. Two young assistants are behind the counter of the well-stocked Frensham post office, located at the Millbridge crossroads.

Rural Recollections
by Monica Jones

ALTHOUGH most of our staple food came from the locality (the 'Best of British' was our watchword, eaten in season), we didn't have to go outside the village for much else that we needed.

There were the butchers and bakers (I'm not sure about the candlestick makers) and small general stores selling everything from sugar and flour to soap and paraffin (the soap we used for scrubbing both clothes and floors was called Sunlight and came in long yellow bars off which chunks were cut). One such shop, called the Ideal Stores, was run by two ladies called Miss Kiel and Miss Twine. I think it was they (I'm not sure about this, but certainly it was two munificent village ladies) who provided the feast for my wedding in 1958 for the princely sum of £10; the memorable cream horns were certainly horns of plenty.

The two butchers slaughtered their own pigs and the bakers baked their own bread and much else

that was delectable. The Mecca for us, of course, as children, was McCarthy's sweet shop. There we bought colour-changing gob-stoppers, aniseed balls and sherbet dabs that came with magical packets of Japanese paper flowers that blossomed in water. And of course 'love hearts' with their never-to-be-imparted secret messages.

On boat-race day in March we bought our Oxford and Cambridge favours there: the dark blue and light blue rosettes or little pipe-cleaner men on pins, before crowding breathlessly round the wireless set to listen to the heart-stopping contest. We were Oxford, our friends Cambridge, and afterwards the victors were expected to throw a party for the losers. It always seemed to be Oxford then; we decorated the table with swathes of royal blue crêpe paper and chimney sweep's brushes (grape hyacinths) in jam jars and ate virulently iced fairy cakes.

McCarthy's was also home to the sub-post office.

Later this moved to be twinned with a haberdashery. The sub-postmaster's wife, who sold the colourful range of knitting wools, was sister to the wife of the builder in the village; another sister played the organ in church.

The village on the other side of our farm also boasted a sweet shop and post office in what had been the toll house on the old turnpike road to Guildford. On the opposite side of the road was an early filling station. This was run by the father of our childhood friends. Their grandfather, a builder, had sand

Another village post office, this time at Tongham, advertises the fact that telegrams could be sent from within.

and gravel pits there and in restoring them, was a conservationist before his time. He could often be seen climbing a long ladder up the sand face with his little dog Peter behind him.

His brilliantly inventive son (our friends' Uncle Allan) began his career at the age of 16 by making a machine to manufacture breeze blocks. In the mid-1930s he invented his first tile-making machine and later a more sophisticated version which was taken up by an international company and put into production world-wide.

All kinds of services were on offer in the village. You could have your hair cut in the front room of the part-time barber. Often we three girls had identical dresses (with knickers) made in triplicate by the village dress-maker; these were then handed down, year by year. You could have your bicycle mended or your battery charged, your boots repaired or your chimney swept.

I don't remember a forge in the village, although I know historically there had been several, one as late as the early 20th century, where village children

The man on the left outside this cycle repair workshop is a postman. Has he called to deliver the mail or did he need a repair to speed him on his way? The workshop, located near Farnham, advertises the fact that it can supply BSA parts.

Some villages had a dairy in a shop. In most, however, the milk was supplied direct from a local farm. Here two dairy maids pose outside the milking parlour at Runfold Farm in 1919. One is holding the traditional three-legged stool designed to rest firmly on the most uneven floor. Occasionally such stools only had one leg, to just form a simple 'perch' from which the cow could easily be milked.

took their iron hoops to be mended. There were several coal rounds and the haulage business established in 1910. The founder, then 17, often went without his dinner to buy his first horse and soon had several carters working for him. They had horses and mules, which were replaced by steam engines and petrol lorries in the 1920s.

On the farm, many rural crafts were practised, from hedging and ditching, hop cultivation and drying, to horse and dairy management. The steam-driven threshing machines chugged into the farmyard each autumn. They were hired, but just after the war my uncle bought one of the first tractor-driven threshers and hired this out in his turn. In time, the farm had its own workshop and touring mobile farm shops selling fresh produce.

In earlier times, all our farm waggons were made at George Sturt's wheelwrights nearby in Farnham. My uncle, who visited the shop with his father, describes the hand-built Surrey waggons, as they were called, as 'strong double-shafted waggons, which could be used for all kinds of work, and would last for generations.' Mr Sturt himself went to Alice Holt woods to select the oak trees used for his waggons.

Best of all, I remember the visiting knife-grinder, with his big cart-mounted wheel from which the sparks streamed upwards in dramatic firework-like showers as he sharpened our scissors and scythes and carving knives.

Thursley dairyman Thomas Baker had an early pick-up truck with which to deliver milk to his customers. Here he is collecting milk from Highfield Farm in the village prior to setting off on another day's deliveries.

Going back probably a generation to 1920, these dairy carts are ready for the off at Park Farm Dairy at Badshot Lea. The dairy here was owned by A. Robins, who ran a number of horse-powered businesses in the district around Farnham, from livery stables to removals and general carting. The view was taken by Jimmy Rawlings, a well known local photographer.

For centuries one of the main centres of village life was the mill. Here the farmer took his grain for making into flour or animal feed, and the villagers bought the flour to produce their bread and occasional cakes.

Often the mill was the largest building in the village and the miller held considerable sway in village affairs. This is Richard Budd, the last miller at Cosford Mill, Thursley where he installed a new waterwheel cast in a Reading foundry.

When milling ceased at Thursley, Richard moved to High Salvington in West Sussex and learnt a new craft, for unlike the watermill at Thursley, High Salvington's was powered by the wind.

Illustrating why the mill was such an important building in the local scene are these two striking examples. Above is Overy Mill at Dorchester-on-Thames in Oxfordshire. It appears, from the mill races, that this had two waterwheels, meaning it would have had at least four sets of millstones.

Most mills suffered fire damage at least once during their working lives. Small quantities of flour mixed with air, a situation that could easily have occurred throughout the mill, formed a very explosive mixture, which could be ignited by the smallest spark or heat from poorly lubricated bearings.

Newark Mill, *(below)* was almost totally destroyed by fire in 1966. It was located near the ruins of Newark Priory in Pyrford near Woking, alongside the Wey Navigation, which provided easy transport for its products. Parts of the structure dated from the mid-17th century and in its heyday, eight pairs of stones were worked by three waterwheels.

Most mills, however, were not so fortunate as Newark in having such good transport close to hand. Headley Mill, near Bordon in Hampshire, is shown in these two photographs illustrating alternative means of getting raw materials and the product to market.

The cart is delivering grain to the mill, which specialised in flour and animal feeds. This would probably have come from a local farm, so the journey would not have been too long. The outgoing flour, however, generally had to travel to a wider market. Thus the introduction of steam power was a great improvement. The lower photograph shows a steam lorry which has travelled from Erith in Kent to collect the mill's products.

Headley Mill is now a rare survivor in that it still contains all its original machinery in working order and is occasionally put to use. It is also capable of generating its own electricity supply.

Few villages are fortunate enough to boast a hospital. Cranleigh, between Godalming and Horsham, is claimed to be the largest village in England and it does have a hospital. In 1859 a cottage was offered, rent free, to the rector, and this became the first cottage hospital in the country. It is still open in this age of centralisation, and small surgical procedures can be performed there.

Many of the woodland crafts of the countryside were carried out in the coppices that supplied the raw material. However, some craftsmen preferred to work in a village. Today many of these craftsmen come together at the Rural Life Centre each year on the last Sunday in July, Rustic Sunday, to demonstrate their skills.

Here a besom maker bundles birch twigs to make the traditional country broom still much appreciated by gardeners. Besoms were also made using heather from the surrounding heaths, but these did not last as long as the birch variety.

Timber of all forms was much in demand throughout the country for building and many other purposes, from wheelwrighting to coopering. This photograph shows the staff of Tongham sawmill with a huge pile of sawn boards and some of the tools they would have used to make them. Felling and hand axes, circular and cross-cut saws plus spanners to adjust the machinery are all visible. Because of its proximity to the developing Aldershot Camp, much of the production probably went into the new barrack blocks being built when the photograph was taken.

Joinery workshops were often situated on the upper floors of buildings in order to provide better lighting for the carpenters working within. These men are the staff of Goddards in East Street, Farnham, and their windows, doors and staircases, among many other items, were built into houses over a wide area.

The coming of mechanisation to the rural world demanded a source of power that could be easily moved about the farm to drive the new equipment. Many small engineering firms sprang up in the country towns, often in former blacksmiths' premises. Some produced engines of their own design while others bought in powerplants which they re-sold and serviced.

George Parfitt's works were in West Street, Farnham, and pictured here is the company's stand at a local agricultural show. George Parfitt is second from the right, at the back, and Ernie Fosbery is on the extreme right.

A page from an equipment catalogue advertises the products of the Hornsby company from Grantham in Lincolnshire. The firm were keen to point out that their products were easy to operate.

Young Jack Vick seems very proud of this machine at his home in Badshot Lea. It is a vertical-boilered, double-acting steam engine with governor control. Note the heavy weight on the safety valve. The drive could be taken from the flywheel to all manner of machinery.

Another of John Henry Knight's accomplishments was the invention of the first paraffin oil engine. Here an example of his engine is seen driving a chaff cutter in around 1890. It is thought that this photograph was taken for publicity purposes, to promote his patented design. Another version was developed to provide electric light for country houses.

Chapter 4
Time Off

FOR MANY country dwellers much of their time away from work was spent just living. Cooking, cleaning and tending the garden all took a lot of this 'free' time. Then of course there were repairs to tools and clothing - there was little spare cash to purchase new items.

However, there was time to relax and the rural community had their own special ways of making the most of it as we shall see. But the countryside was everyone's playground, especially with the arrival of better transport be it bus, bike or car. These two young ladies have brought their picnic to the meadows beside this old watermill.

Judging by the china tea service, they arrived by

car and their dress would tend to indicate they came from a town. However we don't know the location though it is thought to be somewhere in Sussex.

The mill is typical of so many in this part of the country that fell out of use as commercial roller mills in the cities took over much of the flour production needs of the country.

The two ladies from the previous photograph, after they had finished their refreshments, obviously decided to explore their surroundings. After a paddle in the water they pose for the third member of their party perched on the frame of the weir that controlled the flow of water to the mill wheel.

Back in Victorian times a walk in the country was a popular pastime, especially if there was a romantic ruin as the goal. The date of this photograph is around 1880 and it was taken by John Henry Knight.

At the time the Knight family lived at Weybourne, just outside Farnham. About an hour's walk away was Waverley, a tiny hamlet with an interesting cave in which a witch was supposed to have lived, and the ruins of a Cistercian abbey. Behind the young lady is the former monks' refectory, then very overgrown by creepers. Today the ruin is under the protection of English Heritage. The damaging vines have been removed and the meadow is kept mown. Somehow though, the ruins no longer seem quite so romantic.

Walking in the country for town dwellers brought them in touch with another world. The photograph above was taken by Major Lane of Rowledge and shows a very well-dressed walker in the middle of a local farm. He has paused to study his surroundings and ponder things he possibly does not fully understand.

The ladies below, however, have the benefit of some expert local knowledge. They have come across a shepherd and his flock on the Downs. Is he telling them about his work or just showing them the correct way to their destination?

Probably 80 years separate these two photographs, yet the subject matter is the same: lunchtime during the harvest. Above the workers on the Tilford House estate, only a few hundred yards from the Rural Life Centre, pause from the task of hay making. Liquid refreshment, probably ale, is being handed out and most have squatted where they stopped. In the background is the summer house, which still stands today.

Below, two members of a harvesting crew at Bentley during the 1950s sit down on a bale and enjoy cups of tea (or possibly coffee) from their vacuum flasks. They have brought their tractor and baling machine into the field to follow the combine harvester, which cut the crop and separated the grain.

The baler picked up the straw and packed it into neat bales, which were then stacked ready for another tractor and trailer to collect. Back at the farmyard, the bales would be stacked in an open-sided building or in a rick to keep them dry for use in the animal stalls during the winter months.

The appearance of the bicycle truly liberated the working man and woman. As well as providing a cheap to run means of travelling further to find work, it allowed them to venture further in their leisure time. These two, in their Sunday best, are visiting Millbridge at Frensham. They have stopped outside the post office where the postmaster, Mr Sturt, had their photograph taken. If the photograph had been taken today, they could well be on their way to visit the Rural Life Centre, which is but half a mile along the road that disappears off to the right.

This intrepid group of early cyclists are believed to have been photographed by John Henry Knight in around 1895. They are posed in front of a thatched cottage in Selborne which still looks the same today, and are members of the Farnham Road Club. The road club is still going strong and today organises time trials along the Alton road from Farnham, the same route by which these cyclists may well have travelled.

Almost 30 years later, the old toll house in Runfold on the other side of Farnham became a popular spot for cyclists, illustrated by the Cyclists' Touring Club sign hanging from the wall. Some of them, too, may well have been members of Farnham Road Club. The reason for its popularity was, of course, because this end of the building had been turned into a café. It soon outgrew the premises, however, and a purpose-designed wooden building had to be erected in the garden.

Another interesting spot for the cyclists to have stopped on their tour, had they been riding in 1955, would have been this gundog trial at Elstead. It is early May and the leaves have yet to appear on the trees. However, the hard-working dogs are expected to plunge into the cold River Wey to recover the retrieve under the watchful eyes of the judges.

Perhaps a rather controversial subject these days, fox hunting was once very important in providing leisure for the gentry and a welcome source of extra employment for the lower classes. This photograph shows the meet of the Hampshire Hunt in spring 1953 at Crondall. The village's striking church is visible through the bare outline of the lime trees which form an avenue to its door.

Even more controversial, and today very much against the law, the Courtney Tracey otter hounds gather on the banks of the River Wey at Millbridge, Frensham with the Mariners Inn in the background. This was in April 1956. Today the otter is a protected species and a great rarity in our streams and rivers, although there are signs that it is making a comeback.

Frensham Ponds, both Little and Great, have always proved a popular destination for town and city dwellers on summer weekends. Today both are owned by the National Trust, which is rather restrictive about the activities allowed around and on the water. Back at Easter 1957, however, the boats at the Little Pond, run by Mr Atherton the then owner, were very popular, as were the tea rooms on the shore. Today the buildings form a home for the National Trust warden. The area was also widely used, and still is, for military training. In the background can be seen a former World War Two barrage balloon, used for giving trainee members of the Parachute Regiment, then based in Aldershot, their first jumps.

The year 1956 saw a particularly severe winter, and the Great Pond was frozen over enough to provide a safe skating rink through to late February. There are even stories of cars being driven onto the ice. Our milder winters today mean that such sights are now a rarity.

In the early years of the 20th century hard winters seem to have been the norm. Here in 1908 Badshot Lea village pond has frozen over and formed an extra playground for young and old alike. The lads seem to be equipped for a rudimentary game of ice hockey, probably using ice as a puck.

Beyond lie the school on the left and the church with the village crossroads between them. The photograph was taken by Jimmy Rawlings, who was a watchmender in the village.

The pond has seen much activity over the years and has now been restored as a nature reserve. However, at around the turn of the 19th century it was used as punishment for a wife beater. He was dragged through the water by the village women. When asked why he was not 'taking charge' the village bobby proclaimed that 'as long it was only women doing it' he wouldn't interfere.

The church has always had a profound and wide influence on all aspects of country life, not least in the villagers' leisure time. Here the Revd A.J. Wheeler, vicar of Thursley, is seen with mothers and friends of the 'King's Messengers'. This would appear to be a Mothers Union-like organisation and the group here are probably gathered in the vicarage garden for a social occasion.

Horses have brought this Church Army caravan to Shortfield, Frensham during the early years of the 20th century. This organisation, based in Edgware, London, sent these 'mission' caravans around the country to offer support to the working man and woman, particularly the itinerant workforce that travelled from place to place as the seasons passed.

Another photograph from Major Lane's collection at the Rural Life Centre shows what is probably a vicarage tea party to raise funds for the church at Rowledge. Nearly everyone is wearing a hat and the gentleman in the left distance is doffing his to the seated ladies.

A church fête, again probably in a vicarage garden, with many village organisations represented, is shown here. Everyone is dressed in their best for this important occasion in the village's social calendar.

At Badshot Lea the Darby and Joan Club is a long-standing institution. Above they gather outside the village's primitive methodist chapel for a photograph in around 1950. They more recently met in the Working Men's Club, but the location of the photograph below was not recorded.

It shows the club's Christmas party in 1957, with Alan Tice conducting the community singing, once a strong feature of many village social events.

Still in Badshot Lea, the top photograph shows lads in the village who played cricket on the village green in around 1910. Beyond are the hop kiln and Badshot House, subsequently demolished during the 1960s. The green is still there and is currently used for boys' football. The adults play on the adjacent recreation ground.

However, at Tilford the village green is still very much the centre of local sport and has now a well-tended cricket pitch, which draws a large crowd on fine summer weekends. When this photograph was taken in the 1870s, however, sheep were still allowed to graze on the pitch between games. Some can be seen in front of the Barley Mow public house, which was and still is popular with players and spectators alike.

Despite the relaxed way the village looked after its pitch, it housed one of the most famous cricketers of his day. In the bungalow next to the large oak tree lived 'Silver Billy' Beldham, who was the doyen of other local players. His house, where he retired to make bats after many years in Wrecclesham, has had a second storey added, but its famous one-time occupant is not remembered on the building.

Chawton Football Club poses for the photographer after a successful 1932–33 season. The village, near Alton, is better known for its Jane Austen connection.

Rural Recollections
by Monica Jones

ONE OF MY earliest memories is (appropriately enough, as a hop-grower's daughter) my first taste of beer.

I was about three years old and in my hazy recollection, the occasion must have been an end of harvest supper, with the farm-workers sitting round the big table in the kitchen, replete and jovial. I was lifted onto the table to sing (in a voice, I'm sure, about as chirrupy as the crickets behind the black-leaded stove) for a sip of the strong stuff; in those days, Dinner Ale was one of the products of the local breweries.

Puttenham farmer Sam Marshall writes about the harvest suppers he knew at the end of the 19th century: 'The happiest and jolliest time came when the harvest was all gathered in – the harvest supper, when all the men and women, united with their master, enjoyed a hearty meal of roast beef and plum pudding on the big floor of the hop-kiln. The labourers' wives set their brick ovens and their coppers to work to cook for these hearty men, women and lads.

'After the supper the farmer would say a few words of thanks and would then be called upon to sing the first song... Everyone would join in these old ballads and make merry.' Among the songs (Sam himself knew 50 of them) were *We are all jolly boys that follow the plough* and *John Barleycorn*, but the greatest favourite of them all was *The Farmer's Boy*.

Harvest suppers continued in most villages until well into the 20th century (as I well knew from my *Herald* experience) and are still going strong in some. The churches took over the role of host,

Young tennis players of the Tice family on their Runfold court.

inviting the whole community as an adjunct to harvest thanksgiving. The jollity was still intrinsic, and I remember the fun of the speeches and 'turns'.

The end of 'hopping' was another excuse for letting the hair down. A treatise on Farnham hops, written in 1798, describes these Finishing Frolics: 'The pole-puller has not a handkerchief only, but also a shirt (that is, a piece of linen cloth to make him one) given him by the pickers. This is worn, sash-wise, and is ornamented with ribbons.

'The women, likewise, decorate themselves with such handkerchiefs, ribbons and finery as they purchase at the shops to carry home with them. Some of the companies parading the streets of Farnham, perhaps with a fiddler at their head, singing and shouting in tones of true licentiousness; the evening being usually closed by a dance, and always with copious libations – doubtless to the goddess of hops.'

Even in the 1930s, when I was a girl, there was this 'school is out' feeling as the hop-pickers lined up for their pay at a table set up outside the kiln. Women who had worn their flowered cotton aprons day after

Action on a sunny afternoon in 1957 at Rowledge, as the home team meets the bowling side from Seale and Sands. About to bowl on the far rink is Kit Doward. Just beyond her is the back of the village's cricket pavilion.

day as a protection against the black hop stain put on their best clothes and there was much ribald banter as they tossed the pole-pullers into the air on the hop sacks or up-ended them in the seven-bushel baskets.

For us, the end of hopping meant the end of searching for hop dogs (the fat, hairless green caterpillars) and king hops – outsize hops spiked with leaves – and rides to the kilns on waggons piled with the redolent sacks, there to bake potatoes in the furnaces.

In November, the spent hop bines were burnt on a huge bonfire in the farmyard to which the whole village was invited, with barrels of beer, bread and

Besides the church the other centre of village social life was the public house. These two are typical of such establishments, one large, the other small. Above is the Barley Mow at The Sands, probably photographed during the 1900s. Outside are some of the regulars. From left to right: Bill Guppy, Jim Birchett, Walt Lunn the landlord, Fred Birchett, Sid Alexander, Charlie Fry, Shiner Knight, Ernie Gardner and Bill Elkins.

Below is the Cricketers, which stands close to the crossroads at the centre of Badshot Lea, surprisingly quite a distance from the village's cricket pitch. The date is 1905 and the soldier is Harry Wilkinson. Looking out of the window is the Ernie Langridge, the landlord's son.

cheese and pickled onions, fireworks and a torchlight procession.

The village played as hard as it worked; the pubs and the Working Men's Club were the social centres, and there were the various sports clubs, cricket, tennis and football (nicknamed the Dockers from the local propensity to flood). But the only ship to come out of the village was the *Saucy Kipper*, the prizewinning entry in a 1904 carnival and again in the 1950s.

There was always plenty of acting talent in the village, the Women's Fellowship wowing the local concerts with their spirited sketches. There was musical talent too; long before my time, however, the temperance band came to an ignominious end when a quack doctor called Sequaw drove into town accompanied by a band of 'Red Indians', whose war-cries drowned the yells of the brave-hearts whose teeth he proceeded to pull; he also sold a cure-all called Prairie Oil.

Sequaw organised a band competition and the temperance stalwarts won. Unfortunately, the prize was a case of whisky which was opened on the spot, and when the unsteady bandsmen returned to the village, their instruments were confiscated.

The farmers themselves organised rabbit and pheasant shoots (especially on Boxing Day), beagling for hares and otter hunts. As a *Herald* reporter, I attended the last otter hunt held on the River Wey, though I don't think the whisker of an otter was seen for long before that.

Fairs regularly visited the village (I used to climb out of my bedroom window to go to them). As teenagers, we went into town to the 'flicks', to see Will Hay in *Oh, Mr Porter* and *The Ghost Train*, Deanna Durbin, Jeanette Macdonald and Nelson Eddy, and Rogers and Astaire. But in the main, the village was as self-contained in its entertainment as in everything else. There were the weekly 'hops' in the Scouts' Hut (I danced there with New Zealand and Canadian soldiers during World War Two) and summer fêtes in the Parsonage garden.

At the Christmas bazaars in the Mission Hall (once a dame school and then used for services before the church was built), the basins of delectable, spicy, jelly-laced brawn made by my mother were quickly sold; for me, the revolting smell of the pigs' heads boiling up in preparation evoked the first anticipatory promise of Christmas.

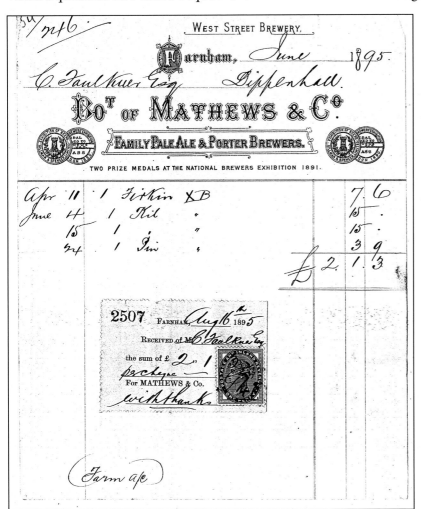

A brewer's invoice from 1895, issued by the West Street brewery in Farnham, then run by Mathews. This particular one was not issued to a pub, however, it was for a supply to Mr Faulkner of Dippenhall, just outside the town, and charged to his 'farm account'.

The ale would probably have been supplied to the farm workforce and formed part of their wages. How would a modern Inland Revenue inspector interpret this 'benefit in kind?'

Of particular interest are the measures used, peculiar to the brewing industry. They are firkins, kilderkins and pins. Also Mr Faulkner was not a rapid payer: the receipt sticker, with one penny stamp duty, is dated 16 August, almost two months after the bill was issued.

These two views show regulars enjoying themselves within the Barley Mow at The Sands during the 1950s. The landlord and his wife are Ariel and Mrs Towns. On the other side of the bar are, from left to right, Reg Rhymes, Ernie Smith and Herbert Gardner.

Reg also appears in the centre of the photograph below playing a game of cards with Charlie Beeson and Fred Beagley. Note that beer glasses are apparently not allowed on the card table.

In the background is what could easily be mistaken for the screen of a video game machine. However, this is the 1950s and the item is in fact an electric fire, propped up on another table to keep the players warm.

The Royal Huts Hotel at Hindhead was very much used to catering for 'passing trade'. This was situated alongside the main London–Portsmouth road, so travellers of all sorts stopped here for refreshment, from the sailors who used to walk back to their ships to the coach parties on a day trip to the seaside.

The inn was at a busy crossroads so dealt with local trade as well, especially on market days. The hotel, for that is what it became following a complete rebuild, remained popular for a very long time. However changing tastes finally caught up with it and it became a Happy Eater family restaurant. This conversion was unsuccessful, possibly through no fault of its own because the traffic outside was at a standstill for much of each day as the road got busier and busier. When the travellers eventually arrived at the crossroads, the last thing they wanted to do was stop again for refreshment. They would rather get on with their delayed journey.

Now the building has been totally demolished, and the site will become just another housing development.

Gone, it seems, are the days of the local friendly societies that helped the workers save and looked after their welfare. The pub was always their preferred meeting place and here the Seale Friendly Society is assembled outside the Victory Inn, which once stood on the Hogs Back between Farnham and Guildford, where it passed close to the village centre.

The pub was swept away in one of many successive road widenings, and it, like the society and its magnificent banner, is gone for good.

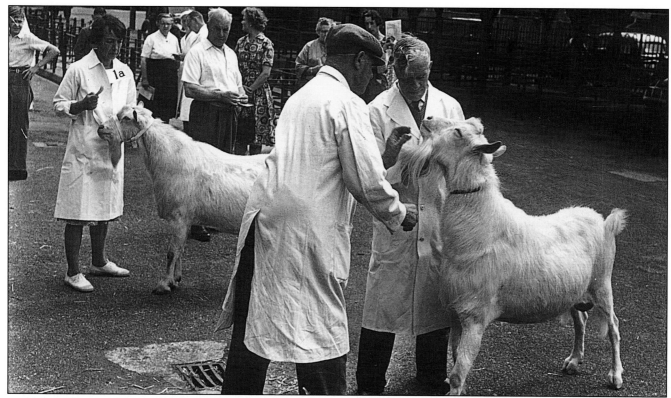

Farmers not only regarded their animals as their work, they were also proud of them and took great pains to ensure that they were in the best of health and condition. Regular competitions were held to allow them to compete for the best animal of a breed each year.

Here, in the confines of the Farnham cattle market, the keepers have brought along their charges for the Surrey & Hants Male Goat Show in June 1959. The 'billy' in the foreground certainly seems to be enjoying the occasion.

The horses on a farm were particularly valued. Before the introduction of the steam engine and the tractor they were the primary source of motive power, whether for driving machinery or pulling ploughs and waggons.

Farmers, ploughmen and carters were always proud of their powerful companions and took great pains to ensure that they always looked their best, even when working on the farm. Ploughing matches were held each year to determine the best ploughmen of the district. These events always also had a harness class for the best turned out pair. This handler is at a match in the Cranleigh area during the 1960s.

This is the North East Hants Ploughing Match, held on Hall Farm at Selborne in October 1954. Such events always drew, and still draw, many spectators, all of whom cast an 'expert' eye over the work of each ploughman and the occasional ploughwoman. In the background the ricks of the crop harvested earlier from these fields await the arrival of the threshing gang.

Tractors, too, took part in ploughing matches but somehow lacked the charisma of the horse teams. The lack of spectators at this Guildford & District match during 1959 is evidence of this fact. Perhaps the perception was that the tractor, like this Fordson Major Diesel, was easier to control to make a straight furrow than a pair of shire horses at full tilt.

Epitomising the community spirit that pervaded all village life is this wonderful photograph of swing boats brought annually to stand outside the Primitive Methodist chapel at Badshot Lea for the children to enjoy.

Mr Barnes brought his ride the three miles from Aldershot and erected it here, alongside the main road through the village. This is the same chapel that the Darby and Joan Club assembled outside for their portrait featured earlier in this chapter.

THE AREA covered by this book had more than its fair share of large country estates, probably as a result of its proximity to London. Many well-to-do families had more than one such house and progressed around the country during the year. They often took a large proportion of their personal staff with them but gardeners were usually employed from the local villages as the grounds needed constant attention whether the family were 'in residence' or not.

Here the gardeners at Moor Park House just outside Farnham pose for the photographer toward the end of the 19th century. The young child looks too well dressed to be the garden boy, so it is likely he was a member of the owner's family. The hierarchy of the garden staff was denoted by their dress and the hats they wore, with the senior members wearing bowler hats.

The country houses provided another source of employment for many, whether directly on the staff or in one of the businesses supplying the family's needs.

Moor Park House has had an illustrious past, having once belonged to Sir William Temple, who employed Jonathan Swift. Mr Swift was the author of *Gulliver's Travels,* which he wrote while in residence here, and a few years back large murals were discovered beneath the wallpaper in the ballroom depicting scenes from Gulliver's adventures in Lilliput and Brobdingnag.

Huge amounts of money were invested in the grounds of the country houses and even modest homes had spectacular settings. This is the artificial lake created at Wishanger Lodge in Frensham. The lodge was basically a wooden structure that probably cost far less than the creation of its setting.

Most estates had their own plant nurseries where decorative and food plants were brought on to supply family, guests and the small army of servants. However, the demand for ever more exotic plants led to expeditions around the world to seek out previously undiscovered species and a rise in the importance of the commercial nursery. These nurserymen, perched among their prize blooms, are at Chalcraft's Nursery in Dorking in around 1900. Behind them stretch the glasshouses so vital for propagating these delicate plants.

Rural Recollections
by Monica Jones

I WAS BORN in a four-square Surrey farmhouse with a solid Victorian frontage on a much older, possibly single-storey, rear, into which my grandfather (son of a Puttenham hopgrower) moved in the 1880s with his bride, whose father was an Alton brewer.

In my teens, my home was a modest gabled house – with a moat. Foxes raised their cubs in the bank, kingfishers nested there and a crusader's medallion was found at the bottom of a well in the garden. This was the site of a long-gone mansion, Badshott Place, once the home of Peckham Williams who introduced the white bine hop – the prestigious Farnham hop – which gave beer a reputedly unrivalled flavour and Farnham its fine Georgian houses.

Charles I, en route to the gallows, and diarist James Boswell, whose daughter was staying there, are both recorded as visiting Badshott.

Nearby are Weybourne House, Badshot Farm and Barfield, at various times associated with inventor (of early motor cars and much else) John Henry Knight. John Henry gave popular lantern lectures about his inventions and set up a 'Lads' Institute' in a local hop kiln.

One popular pastime was making fireworks, which came to an abrupt end when two firecrackers were thrown into the back of a trap driven by the Farnham police superintendent.

There was a clutch of big houses in Runfold; one, Whiteways End, was once the home of Miss Courtauld, whose family were famed as textile manufacturers, patrons of the arts and generous benefactors. Wearing a poke bonnet and smocked dress, I once presented a bouquet to her when she opened a village bazaar. Other big houses housed Land Army girls and New Zealand troops during World War Two.

The two really great houses close by were Waverley Abbey House and Moor Park House. Waverley Abbey House was the home of the Anderson family, visited by Florence Nightingale, who was the niece of former owners the Nicholsons. It was a distinguished nursing home for convalescent army officers during the two world wars, presided over by Mrs Rupert Anderson and three of her four nursing daughters (the fourth was in France). The Andersons had lived at Waverley for over 70 years when, in 1939, Major and Mrs Rupert Anderson celebrated their golden wedding. Over 600 local people subscribed to the gift of an

Bill Etherington, on the left of this photograph, always claimed he was born under a holly bush on Puttenham Common, and lived all his life at Pot Common, Elstead. He worked as a copse cutter and started his own business, which became very successful, employing about a dozen men.

The team used horses and carts to transport the timber and the split hazel produced was used by Jack Turvil of Puttenham for making hurdles. Much of Bill's time was spent working on the Hampton Estate at Seale, owned by Richard (later Sir Richard) Thornton, to whom he is talking here. Frequently Bill would continue working into the night, using just a candle attached to a branch for illumination as he split the hazel rods.

engraved silver-gilt coffee set and as well as the group family photograph, there was one of old family servants, six of them with over 50 years' service.

Across the artificial lake with its water lilies and herons, where a jewelled scabbard was found in the mud during a drought in the 1960s, is ruined Waverley Abbey, England's first Cistercian monastery – a mysterious magical place visited by deer in the evenings. It is now opened by English Heritage to the

This group of 'girls' were in service with a family from Clandon near Guildford. They travelled with the family on holiday to Crows Nest at Sea View in the Isle of Wight where the photograph was taken in July 1922. Front left is Anne Pearl and her sister May is on the right of the back row.

Another gardening team, this time from Snowdenham Hall at Bramley, in around 1894. Assembled in front of a carriage, the senior man gets to sit down while Albert Ashdown, on the left and then in his twenties, who was in charge of the greenhouses, has to stand.

public, but when I was young it was privately owned and only briefly and tantalisingly glimpsed from the woods on the other side of the river.

But we often passed Moor Park House, with the old droveway going through the drive within feet of the front door, equally romantic with its associations with Jonathan Swift, who was a secretary there, and his beloved Stella (said to have lived at a cottage nearby). And within yards there

were the caves of the legendary Mother Ludlam and Father Foot (who, we were deliciously told, had walked the streets of Farnham in living memory, wearing a big black cloak).

We used to creep as far as we could go into sandy Mother Ludlam's cave, where a duck was once said to have been launched on the underground stream, coming out featherless at Guildford.

We swooped to Moor Park on our bicycles on the

A really big estate staff here, photographed sometime during World War Two at Churt. This is the Bron-y-De estate of former prime minister David Lloyd George. He has white hair and is seated near the centre of the group.

Lloyd George was an active and enthusiastic farmer, always one of the first to try out new ideas. During the war much of the land was handed over to help the war effort and many Women's Land Army members were drafted in to help from sowing to harvest. Some of the Land Girls, in their uniforms complete with ties, are seated at the front of the group.

Many estates were used for shooting parties and the gamekeeper was a very important man in the district. He could hire and fire the staff he needed to ensure there were adequate targets for the 'guns' once November came.

To supply the birds required, a whole new industry sprang up as is evidenced by this advertisement for pheasant and partridge eggs from the Liphook Game farm.

switchback road through the pine woods; once I daringly called at the big house when I was collecting for the Red Cross. It was still privately owned (it later became a Christian college and then a girls' finishing school). The door to the marble-floored, glass-fronted lobby was opened by a white-coated, white-turbanned Indian who seemed at least seven feet tall. Too awe-struck to speak, I held out my Red Cross tin.

He did not speak either; he just turned and vanished, leaving the door open. Uncertainly, I waited until at last he returned, carrying a silver salver on which reposed a sixpence. I put it in my tin and went, still wordless; I don't think I even said thank you.

I have a later, deeply affectionate memory of a big house, and that is of Binsted Wyck, near Alton. When I came back after the war, to work for the *Herald*, I made an annual pilgrimage – as did many others – to the magical gardens that Lady Violet Bonham-Carter opened each February so the public could enjoy the marvellous sweeps of winter aconites and snowdrops. She lived then in only part of the great house with its tattered and faded curtains and its motto over the gateway 'Manners Maketh Man', wrapped in its splendid evocation of a gracious and timeless past.

I took my mother there when she was over 90. On one of the overgrown paths of that crumbling, enchanted garden we came on the small figure of Lady Violet, then herself in her 90s, busily sweeping up leaves in preparation for the influx of visitors.

She stopped work to show us the tiny mauve and white winter cyclamen given to her on a diplomatic visit with her husband to Italy; her garden was, like every true garden, full of a lifetime's memories, and there was always wine for her guests at the reception before each year's opening.

Here a shooting party, complete with beaters, assembles for the official photograph outside the Keeper's lodge in Moor Park near Farnham in around 1900. Beating was another reason why local children were absent from school. The families welcomed the extra cash, although looking at the young faces in this photograph some of those involved were not too keen on the assorted game collected at their feet.

While the men and boys were out stalking on the estate the women and younger children usually undertook more gentle and relaxed pastimes such as touring the grounds, either on foot or in some form of animal-powered transport.

Here Knight family children and nannies at Barfield House, Runfold are about to set out for a jaunt in the donkey cart. Many people are surprised at the work a donkey is capable of. The donkey is an ancient beast of burden, but is largely kept as a pet today.

All the photographs on these two pages are connected with the Knight family and were probably taken by John Henry himself. Elizabeth Knight, John Henry's wife, is seen here in her trap in around 1890.

A far grander transport this time for a visitor to the Knight household at Weybourne House. This is the carriage and coachman of the Bishop of Winchester, who at the time lived at Farnham Castle, barely four miles away.

The same wall and gates as in the last photograph identify the location as Weybourne House again, but the transport is in a different league. John Henry was a keen amateur inventor and was always at the forefront with his use of new technology.

This is his steam carriage of 1868, a modified model and still not terribly successful. On one occasion the chain broke and the vehicle ran for nearly half a mile downhill, there being no brake. It was stopped eventually when John Henry ran a wheel into a ditch to slow it before turning it into the hedge, breaking the steering gear.

John Henry Knight went on to design his own internal combustion powered car, the fourth to run on British roads. This still exists in the National Motor Museum at Beaulieu. It worked reasonably well for a number of years but John Henry eventually decided to buy the Benz that he and the family are riding in here. This photograph was taken at Barfield House, Runfold, which the Knights moved to after Weybourne.

George, one of the Knight children, tries out one of his father's other inventions, the 'Trike'. This used the single original front wheel from the car he designed before it was converted to a four-wheel layout. Other parts had even more interesting origins. The exhaust manifold was a Bath Oliver biscuit tin.

Much more sophisticated vehicles at Jenkyn Place, Bentley, complete with their chauffeurs, including Thomas Willoughby Shepheard in the centre. These cars and their drivers went all over the country and even overseas with their owners. Obviously much time was spent in keeping the vehicles in tip-top condition and even the driveway does not have a speck of dirt on it.

Of course when all these magnificent houses were being built, they provided much work for long periods for the local builders. Here a team from Warrens builders poses on the front step of Stovolds Hill at Dunsfold where they have just been working.

Mills Builders of Longbridge in the centre of Farnham worked on many of the large houses erected in the surrounding district as well as other prestigious public buildings. Among the latter was the new Roman Catholic church, St Joan of Arc in Tilford Road.

Here they are grouped in front of the main doors as work progresses in 1929. Note the temporary light railway track laid in the foreground to help the movement of raw materials on such a large project. Fourth from the left in the back row is Charlie Dexter of Lower Weybourne Lane, who was 19 when the photograph was taken.

Chapter 6
The Farmer's Lot

THIS PHOTOGRAPH epitomises most people's view of country life. An idyllic harvesting scene is set against a beautiful view. This early Massey-Harris combine harvester is working at Binsted, between Alton and Farnham, in August 1958.

Machines such as these were the first real labour-saving devices for the modern farmer. Admittedly reapers and binders had helped cut the workload but the crop had still to be gathered up by hand and transported back to the farmyard for threshing in the autumn or winter. However, large numbers of seasonal labourers were still required and there was a limit to what could be achieved in a day.

Up until the mid-1950s the farmer's lot was still very much determined by the weather and the daily workload achievable before the weather changed. Fields remained the size they had been since late medieval times and each farm consisted of numerous small fields grouped around the buildings.

Mechanisation changed all this. The combine could cut the crop and separate the grain all in one operation, and much more quickly. Fields could be larger and situated further from the farm. Less labour was needed despite the larger area covered and the yields began to increase.

Farms grew in size by taking over land from the neighbouring properties. The farms that lost land became homes for urban commuters and many local people had to travel to the towns to seek work. This was really the beginning of rural areas becoming places for relaxation as opposed to places of work for the majority, and tourism soon took over as the most important factor in the rural economy.

Men like George Retalick driving this machine and Jim Knight behind him some would argue were the lucky survivors in this second agricultural revolution. Others would say they were unfortunate as they still endured the far from easy farmer's lot.

The farming year really began in the autumn with the ploughman turning the soil from the previous season's crop. This broke up the soil, exposing it to the winter's frosts, killing weeds and allowing air and moisture to permeate deeper. Here John Baker stands in the furrow behind his horse team and plough at Highfield Farm, Thursley.

Another John Henry Knight photograph, taken on his land at Badshot Farm, shows a Ransomes, Sims and Jeffries plough in use in around 1890. Behind the hedge pole hops can be seen growing.

Harry Davis has almost completed ploughing this field with his trusty team of horses and single furrow plough. This was the last team of horses to work on Stovolds Cross Farm at Shackleford near Godalming.

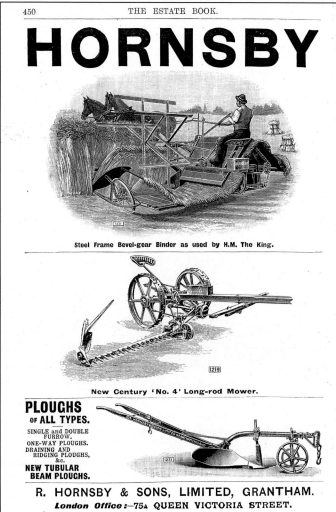

The very latest in farming technology at the time is shown in R. Hornsby and Sons' advertisement in the Estate Book. The firm, located in Grantham, Lincolnshire, could supply machines for use in all the farming seasons.

A horse plough needed almost constant adjustment to match the terrain it was working on. Note the spanner stowed in its holder on the handle, always ready to help achieve the perfect furrow. The reaper and binder was a step in the evolution of the combine harvester, but still required a large labour team to collect and stook the sheaves in the field and later thresh the grain.

Once the soil had been prepared, it was time to sow the seed. Here is John Baker again, from Highfield farm at Thursley, with a galvanised seed lip slung across his shoulders. This carried the seed he was sowing and made it easier for him to broadcast the crop more evenly.

Back on Badshot Farm mechanisation was in use by around 1890. This Suffolk-type steerage seed drill was made by Richard Garrett and Sons of Leiston, Suffolk. It could be adjusted to deal with various types and sizes of seed using brushes or rotating cups. The front of the carriage could be steered by the man on the right ensuring the crop was planted in straight rows.

Hay-making was the first time of celebration during the year when a crop could be harvested. Often whole families turned out to help. However, the two men above are employees of John Henry Knight, who are mowing in the fields behind his Weybourne House in the 1890s. The man on the mower is James Pullinger, who later went on to drive Knight's car, one of the first in Britain.

The machine in use below differs very little from the one above despite there being at least 50 years between the two photographs. The location this time is not recorded and whether the two people on the right are assisting in mowing the field or have just stopped for a chat with the farmer and his wife while on a country walk is uncertain.

Once the grass has been cut it needs to dry in order to become hay. The farmer had to choose the time of mowing carefully to ensure there would be sufficient dry weather to allow for cutting, drying and building into weatherproof ricks. If not the hay would rot in the fields.

Before mechanisation, the hay was turned over once or twice in the field by hand after cutting and before collection. The work was not particularly arduous if the weather was warm and often attracted a wide range of people to help, as is shown above. The man in the centre is holding a traditional hay rake made entirely of wood, which was relatively light and easy to handle. These were made in cottage workshops, some of which are still in action today.

Below a hay tedder, or turner, is at work on Tice's Runfold Farm. This may have been quicker and possibly more effective but machines like this removed much of the romance from the countryside while easing the farmer's lot.

Three hay-making scenes separated by the decades but all looking very similar. Above the haysweeps on the left are bringing their loads for stacking on the rick at Tice's farm at Runfold. The elevator is powered by the horse gear just to the right of it. On the extreme right is another hay tedder. Pitchforks are being used to transfer the hay from the sweeps to the elevator in this field which is now part of a sandpit.

Below left, the haycart is being loaded by a team with pitchforks on Shoelands Farm at Seale during the 1950s. A similar scene on an unknown farm is shown below right in a view dating back to the 1900s.

The photographs on these two pages show the effect of introducing mechanisation to the gathering of the harvest. Above a team armed with scythes work their way steadily across the field. Behind them will come more labourers who will tie the cut crop into sheaves and stook them up in small groups.

The stooks make it easier for the waggon to collect the harvest by reducing the number of stops it must make and at the same time protecting the grain if a shower should develop before it can be taken to the rick yard. The men below are pitching the sheaves up onto the waggon at Pitt Farm, Frensham.

The wonderful harvest scene above shows a reaper and binder at work, with the town of Farnham laid out in the valley bottom beyond. This machine cut the crop and gathered and tied the stalks into sheaves before dropping them back to the ground. The following labourers then only had to stook them ready for collection.

On Badshot Farm in the 1890s, however, they only had the forerunner of the machine above. The sail reaper's sweeps pushed the standing crop against the cutter and then dropped the stalks in sheaf-sized groups off the back of the horizontal platform. The sheaves were then hand tied and stooked as shown on the right.

A typical 1950s harvesting scene in fields at Dippenhall from the *Farnham Herald* archives. The corn has been harvested and stooked in the background, and the team are now bringing the sheaves together to build into a rick.

The start of this can be seen in the centre and pitchforks are again being used to add to it. As the rick gets higher the rick ladder, seen to the right, will be needed to reach the top. Eventually a horse-driven elevator may be needed to complete the job. The children seem to be enjoying

themselves, but they are also serving a useful purpose, like the boy leading the horse in the foreground. Again Farnham can be seen in the distance, with Crooksbury Hill on the horizon.

Here the crop is being stacked in the rickyard at Cross Farm, Shackleford. An elevator is being used but the means of powering it cannot be seen. There could be horse gear on the other side of the rick or it could be the horse's successor, the steam engine, or even an early tractor.

Here the elevator is building a rick of threshed straw. The sheaves from an almost dismantled rick in the centre are being fed to the steam-powered threshing machine on Badshot Farm during the 1890s. Another well-thatched rick awaits its turn on the left.

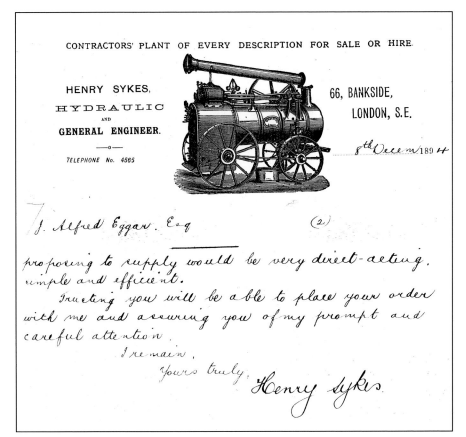

Steam engines were expensive pieces of machinery when first introduced, and many farms hired them in along with the threshing machines they powered. This is the headed notepaper of one such contracting firm based in London dating from 1894. It carried details of a quotation for Farnham farmer J. Alfred Eggar.

John Henry Knight had his own engine and trained one of his estate workers, James Pullinger, to drive it. Here he tends to his charge on Badshot Farm while it powers a threshing set in around 1890. Note the two large containers of water standing by ready to top up the boiler.

Rural Recollections
by Monica Jones

THE FARMER'S lot was always a roller-coaster ride: demanding, unpredictable, heart-stopping. The ups and downs are subject to the relentless whims of the weather, just when things are on the up and up – wham, a late spring frost or a torrential August tips them over onto a downward swoop.

In my early days as a *Herald* reporter in the 1950s, it was my regular job in the 'silly season' of August, when news was scarce, to round up the hop

To protect the harvested crops from the weather until the threshing crew arrived on the farm, the ricks were thatched. Here Ted Langridge is at work on Semaphore Farm in Telegraph Lane at Four Marks, using a rick ladder slightly too long for the job in hand.

and crop prospects. Invariably, the cry was too much rain and too little sun: the corn was laid flat, the hay was rotting in the fields and the hops would not ripen.

My uncle wrote in his memoirs: 'After the shocking prices of 1926, we were hoping for a good year on the farm, but 1927 turned out to be a very wet year. Our hay turned black and was a complete washout. Hop picking was a very wet messy job which took us three weeks.' And '1946 was a terribly wet year and the wettest harvest I have ever experienced; in fact, we did not finish picking up the corn until October 1st and by that time much of it was spoilt. I had one hop garden laid flat during a storm in August, but we were able to gather the hops by cutting off the bines and carrying them to the headland to be picked – a most expensive undertaking.'

A farmer begins his apprenticeship pretty well at birth. My uncle describes how he rode three miles on a small hard-wheeled tricycle to his first school and that 'my out-of-school

Some farms had barns large enough to house the full harvest, as here at Bridge Farm, Runfold. In action is one of the first Ransomes threshing machines, produced just after World War Two. Among the group on the right are Alan Tice, H.E. Fenn, general manager of the West Surrey Farmers Association Ltd, and Jim Tice.

time, holidays and all, were spent happily around the farm, and I learnt all the jobs, harrowing, raking etc., grooming and feeding horses, and I became quite useful and knowledgeable whilst still at school. I never had any doubts in my mind that I too wanted to be a farmer when I grew up.'

In his *Life of a Successful Farmer in Surrey*, Sam Marshall of Puttenham, born in 1864, wrote: 'Starting as a lad, at the age of ten, my first job on the farm was pig-minding on the corn stubbles and rook-scaring, for which I was paid sixpence a day. Schooling was taken in between whiles whenever the farmer could spare me, and I was constantly being taken away from school up to the age of 12, when the education laws came into force insisting that no one should go to work until they had passed their twelfth year.

'From this time on I was employed as a full-time worker on the farm as a plough boy, which meant being up in the morning at five o'clock under a carter with a four-horse team driving the plough... Carter boys at that time were treated very severely. In my early days there were no holidays, or recreations even. If you wanted to go to a cricket match, you had to be up at four in the morning and work up to midday.'

My own grandfather died at the age of 54 in 1908, leaving the responsibility of running the farm (made up of hops, a herd of Shorthorn cows, bullocks for fattening, pigs and chickens, with potato, corn and root crops) to my father, then aged 22. My doughty grandmother had a family of six to bring up – four sons and two daughters. The eldest daughter stayed at home to help run the house. My youngest uncle was then eight.

I had a blissful childhood, but in the recession years of the 1920s and 1930s, the farming life was an agonising struggle. Wonderful crops of hops, corn and potatoes were grown on the farm, but my uncle records that 'the prices for them were so bad that it was almost impossible to earn enough money to pay the wages. Farm labourers got 30 shillings a week, and a carter with two horses to look after got 38 shillings.

'The hops were not sold, but tainted with paraffin and used for manure. We could not sell our potatoes, so we gave a bag away to anyone who would buy a bushel of seed. We could not sell the wheat for milling, so we sold that for poultry at 19 shillings a quarter (4 cwt).

'Well, there it was, starvation for farmers and farm workers alike.'

He goes on to record that '1931 was a chaotic year for everyone. It was wet throughout, and due to the finances of the country being so very grim, the Labour Chancellor ordered a compulsory wage reduction on all salary and wage earners. It was a shocking thing, and one of the worst things that I remember... More than anything else I hated having to hand over, to a skilled man, one pound note and a few shillings for one week's work of fifty hours. How they managed to live I really could not understand.'

At the age of five, I knew nothing of this. But I

A successful year's harvest stooks await collection on Tice's farm during the 1950s.

remember one dramatic and deliciously (for us children) alarming occasion when the hoppickers marched on the farmhouse demanding an extra farthing's pay for each bushel from a field of poor hops.

My father, a genial character affectionately known as 'good old Freddy', had a good rapport with the redoubtable spokeswoman and they were soon exchanging jocular banter. He conceded the farthing, and later took it off again for the better hops – and everyone was happy.

Hops were a very important local crop and their reputation spread far and wide. Farnham hops fetched the highest prices in the 19th century and were much prized. Hop gardens dominated the farming scene, particularly around Alton and Farnham where breweries were established.

Their cultivation required much care and the preparation of the ground was very important. John Henry Knight devised the hop digger shown here in around 1876 to work the gardens which had traditionally been hand dug during the winter months.

A direct-acting machine was not possible because of the soft nature of the ground. This patented device worked by being hauled across the field by a steam engine at the field edge. As well as moving the machine, the drive rope also activated the three forks at the rear and the whole contraption was steered by the man with the tiller.

At first the hops were grown up single poles. This crew are tending to the growing crop. They are applying McDougall's Hop Wash, which they are mixing in the containers on site. The wash was sprayed onto the hops from the narrow-tracked cart partly hidden in the centre of the photograph, which has an arrangement of spray heads at different levels. The driver of this is well protected against the spray by a broad hat and sacking around his shoulders.

In the earlier organic era, pests and diseases were a constant nerve-jangling threat. Hops were always extra disease-prone and a very tricky crop to grow. My grandfather grew damson trees in the farmhouse garden as it was reckoned that blight appearing on them was always a warning that within a few weeks blight would attack the hops. A wash of quassia chips, soft soap, paraffin and soda was got ready for that dreaded day.

The sultry days of June and July threatened blight and downy mildew. Sam Marshall, then retired and well into his 80s, when on holiday in Scotland, sent a postcard to his son during just such a spell of weather, urging: 'Look to the hops, Bill.'

As for the farmer's wife, her responsibility was looking after the poultry, as well as baking and preserving, cleaning and book-keeping, going out into the hop gardens to act as tally man and much, much more. Her perks were the egg money and the profits from the fields of new planted or 'nursery' hops.

Picking of the flowers has just started in this photograph. While most of the crew pose for the camera, a single woman appears hard at work on the right with another partly hidden in the centre. The tally woman stands, pencil poised, to record the quantities produced by each picker.

Pole hops were picked after the poles were lifted from the ground by men with hop dogs, poles with a claw-like attachment on the lower end. This allowed pickers of all ages to reach the crop, as seen in this view of Trimmer's hop garden in Compton, Farnham. Again the tally man is evident near the centre and a waggon is working its way up the field collecting the filled hop sacks.

Whole families would take working holidays in the hop growing areas around picking time to help with the harvest. Here Tony and Iris Jeatt work with their grandmother to fill a picking basket at Puttenham in the late 1940s. The basket formed the measure of quantity, usually seven bushels, that was recorded by the tally man. It was common practise to 'fluff up' the hops in the basket on his approach as his figures determined how much each picker was paid.

Here the tally man is checking the quantities using the official seven bushel measure at Bury Court Farm, Bentley, in 1957. Here the picked hops were transferred from the picking baskets into sacking 'surpluses' for taking to the official measure before being put back into the surpluses for transfer to the kiln. The tally man is S.K. Allen. He recorded the amounts in his own book and on each picker's card.

By this time the hops were being grown on the wire system, which used a permanent framework of poles and wires that were 'strung' each year by a stiltman. The hops then grew up the strings. The pickers pulled down the strings and bines during the harvest. At the edge of the field can be seen the net windbreak which protected the growing bines.

Stripping the bines in the field eventually gave way to machine picking. Here the bines were cut down on to the back of a tractor and trailer and taken straight to the kiln complex on the farm. In a building like this one at Tice's farm, Runfold, the automated picker was installed. This stripped the hop flowers from the rest of the vegetation, which was then mashed up to become a valuable source of manure, or burnt in an annual ceremonial bonfire.

The date of this photograph is September 1955 and the machine shown was introduced that year, replacing two groups of pickers known as the Runfold and Hewitts Gangs, although some pickers were still employed to remove stray leaves from the crop.

On the same farm back in 1919, this waggon belonging to Walter Tice is collecting the surpluses of picked hops for transport to the kiln. In the background pickers can just be seen bundling up the last of these big sacks.

It is at Tice's Runfold Farm in 1919 again that these pickers are emptying their basket into a surplus ready for transport to the kiln. The two younger women on each side are dressed in what looks like World War One Land Army uniform. There was obviously still a shortage of labour following the recent conflict.

To ensure the spiritual wellbeing of the travelling workforce, special missions were set up and visited the picking grounds during the season. This church mission is seen at Bentley in September 1951 and is complete with a barrow-mounted gramophone to accompany their open-air services.

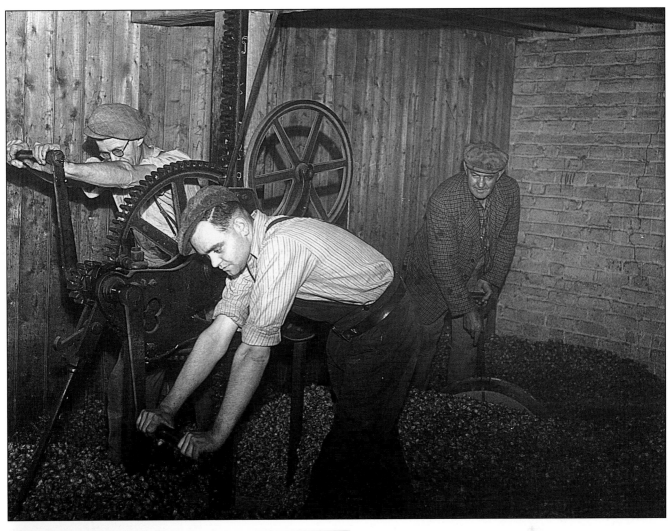

When the hops arrived at the kiln they were dried to prolong their keeping qualities. Sulphur was introduced in the smoke that permeated them in order to kill off some of the bacteria and insects.

Once dried the hops were packed into pockets, or long sacks, each of which weighed one and a quarter hundredweight when full, with the use of a man-powered press. This press was at Weydon Lane, Wrecclesham where George Nash, in the foreground, is using it to pack hops belonging to the Parratt family in 1953.

The hops were gathered with a large 'scuppet' made of bent wood with a canvas or sacking blade, like that being wielded by the man in the background.

Today hops are sold straight to the brewer but in 1919 they were sent to market like most other farm produce. Here a load of well-pressed hop pockets leaves the Runfold kilns in 1919. Traditionally Farnham's hops went to Weyhill Fair near Andover. It was a long journey in the days of horse power, but worth it as the area's hops fetched the highest prices at market.

Some crops required a lot of manual labour to harvest them even when others had been fully mechanised. Potatoes are a good example. Mechanical lifters only unearthed the tubers and pickers were still required to actually recover the crop from among the soil and vegetation, as shown here on Stovolds Cross farm at Shackleford.

HAY PLACE FARM, BINSTED,

Near ALTON, HANTS.

CATALOGUE

OF THE

Live and Dead Farming Stock,

CONSISTING OF

9 USEFUL CART HORSES,

15 3-YEAR-OLD WELSH HEIFERS,

A Quantity of Poultry,

2 WAGGONS, 3 DUNG CARTS,

RAVE AND LIGHT PONY CARTS,

Capital Water Barrel and large Water Tank on Wheels,

REAPING AND MOWING MACHINES,

Manure Drills, Corn Drill, Turnip Cutters, Cake Crushers,

HARROWS, DRAGS, PLOUGHS,

Quantity of Firewood and numerous other Articles, which will be Sold by Auction, on the Premises, by

MR. J. ALFRED EGGAR

On Monday, October 18th, 1875,

At ONE o'clock precisely.

May be Viewed the Morning of Sale, and Catalogues may be obtained at the Bush Hotel, Farnham ; Swan Hotel, Alton, and of the Auctioneer, Swanthorpe Farm, Crondall, near Farnham.

JOHN NICHOLS, Printer, Borough, Farnham.

Perhaps because the life was hard, farms regularly came up for sale through the local auctioneers. Such sales were often regarded as quite a social occasion by the other farmers who tried to ensure the departing family got a fair price for their stock and equipment.

This auction bill of 1875 for Hay Place farm at Binsted near Alton is typical. J. Alfred Eggar was probably the most respected auctioneer in Farnham and the successor to his firm is still in business today.

Farm open days were always popular with the public and drew large crowds, such as this one on a dairy farm near Farnham in the early 1950s. The photograph comes from the *Farnham Herald* archives, now held by the Museum of Farnham.

In the winter the farmer had the land totally to himself and his animals. The scenes can look beautiful in photographs but imagine the hardship suffered by man and animal alike. Peter Watson is leading in his pigs with a trail of food at Stovolds Cross Farm, Shackleford.

On the same farm as the previous photograph the sheep were also having a hard time finding grazing. The farmer erected hurdles to give them a little shelter from the icy blast.

A well wrapped-up shepherd, Bert Belcher, uses a shovel to help reveal the grass beneath the snow. The next step will be to bring in precious hay and expensive processed feeds.

The shire horses familiar on the farm for centuries gave way to the tractor, which only needed 'feeding' when it was actually working.

The early model above is being used to cultivate the soil on Fred Tice's Runfold Farm in the 1920s. That below is moving hay to animals in snow-covered winter fields on Cross Farm, Shackleford. On board the trailer are Percy Boyd, Reg Cray and Ted Hancock, while Albert Watts is driving the Massey-Ferguson tractor.

Contrasting photographs taken on the same farm, Jim Tice's at Runfold, show how the weather could radically alter the farmer's lot.

Workmen are testing the waterlogged soil (*right*) to see if there is any hope of planting a crop, while below the idyllic summer scene shows a successful harvest waiting to be taken to the rick yard and a good crop of grass on the hay meadow, which the cows have just been let into.

The ditch shows evidence of recent work in an attempt to avoid a repeat of the previous scene.

'Horses for courses' in these two photographs and both are farm related. Mrs Ada Tice, *above*, the farmer's wife at Runfold, gets set to run an errand in her pony trap. Below, John Baker and his children, Marjorie and John, stand beside his 1870-built waggon on Highfield Farm at Thursley. Also in the photograph is farm hand Dick Winter.

The horses on all farms were prized possessions, but also regarded as the equals of the human workforce on many. They were well looked after by their handlers and much time was spent in grooming them to always look their best.

These greys on Tice's Badshot Farm were often entered in local shows and ploughing matches where they won many prizes. The team above look ready to set off for such an event as they pose with their human companions in front of the farm's hop kilns. Jim Barrow is on the left.

This team and waggon, *below*, are at an Aldershot Show during the 1950s. Owner Alan Tice stands proudly on the left, the driver is Mr Belton.

Besides the horses, the farmer of yesteryear always valued his largely wooden farm vehicles. They cost a lot to have built, by the standards of the day, and took a long time to manufacture by a small number of skilled wheelwrights.

Because of this, special buildings were often constructed to house the vehicles and implements, like this cart shed at Smallbrook Farm, Thursley. Today's equipment seems far more able to withstand the elements but its useful life is generally much shorter than these wooden masterpieces.

However even these wooden buildings eventually ceased to have any use, either because of deterioration or a change in use of the farm where they were located. The barn shown in the picture below is being demolished, or rather disassembled, on Ivy Hall Farm at Cranleigh in 1887. Much care is being taken and it is most likely that the timbers were re-used in another new building elsewhere and may well still exist. A far cry from today's 'throw away' society, as the farmer's lot still lives on, albeit in a different form.

Chapter 7
Off To Market

THE WEEKLY market was what everyone in the rural community was working towards. It gave them a chance to sell their produce to a far wider audience than the village in which they lived. However, it was far more than this: it provided an important opportunity to meet with fellow farmers, business people and other country folk in general, either to discuss business or just socialise.

The event was important enough to warrant the closing off of entire streets in the town in which it was held. Whole herds and flocks were driven along the country lanes to converge on the market place like this one in North Street, Guildford, during the 1890s.

The occasion was also used by the farmers' wives to visit the shops and buy the necessities of life as well as the very occasional luxury item. However,

note the lack of women in the photograph above.

Besides the general markets such as this one, other specialist fairs existed in some locations dealing solely with a specific commodity. Hops for instance, already mentioned earlier in this book, were traded at Weyhill Fair near Andover in Hampshire. Labour was to be found at hiring fairs held when more hands were taken on for the year.

As food production became more factory based, so the crops went directly to the plant. The markets lost much of their importance and were gradually displaced from the town centres. Today there are few livestock markets left in the country, meaning that farmers wishing to buy and sell animals have to travel vast distances. However, those that do remain are still important social events in the countryside calendar.

Farnham's market was originally held at the foot of Castle Street around the market hall that stood there until the middle of the 19th century *(above)*. Stalls were set up beneath its arcades, the town and its law were administered from the room above and miscreants were housed in cells here too.

Eventually the building, which had fallen into disrepair, was demolished and replaced with the huge corn exchange seen on the right of the photograph below, at the side of the road where its forerunner had stood.

The market continued, along with the huge Farnham Fair held here for two days each year. Then, besides the stalls selling all manner of goods, there were sideshows where all could enter into friendly competition with one another.

Even on non-market days, Farnham's Castle Street still boasted a few stalls at its busy junction with The Borough. This tradition continues today on a piece of land that still belongs to the successor to the company that once owned the old market hall.

Beyond them stands the huge edifice of Lloyds Bank, where the farmers came on market day to deposit the money from the sale of their stock. Parked outside is the first bus in the district, which ran from Hindhead to Farnham via Tilford, and provided a way for the ordinary man and woman to visit the town.

Seen from above, in this 1930s view from the roof of Lloyds Bank, it can be appreciated why Castle Street provided such an ideal venue for the weekly market. Described by some as the finest Georgian street in England, most of the buildings are much older with brick fronts added. Its wide proportions, which could accommodate many stalls and pens, were laid out by a mediaeval bishop. Today its space is occupied by parked cars, but still with ample passage for through traffic up and down the centre.

Farnham's market moved to purpose-built premises in the town's South Street. Here, below the Congregational church spire, the farmers arrived with their lorries and trailers to unload their stock into the pens. This photograph shows pigs being weighed at the opening of the market in 1954.

The same occasion is shown here with pigs and sheep coming under the auctioneer's hammer. This opening followed the rationing of World War Two, when all buying and slaughtering of livestock had been undertaken by the Ministry of Food.

Now private companies were allowed to take over the markets again, Farnham's was run by Messrs Hewett & Lee, with Mr A.V. Lee being the auctioneer in action on the left of this photograph.

The shops around the market also did good trade on market days, often putting on extra displays of their products to attract the weekly visitors. It must have taken the staff of Bundays the butchers in East Street, Farnham, a considerable time to put out this display. It was probably reserved for the peak selling times of the year, like Christmas, and would not be allowed at all today because of the contamination of the meat

from the fumes produced by the passing traffic.

Whether the dog was given the rabbit or helped itself is not recorded.

Advertising products has always been important and it is surprising that what are often thought of as new gimmicks in fact have a long history. Peek Freans used this large bear to promote their Teddy Bear biscuits at the beginning of the 20th century, and it was photographed in the post office and stores at Millbridge, Frensham. Notice that the shop is also selling Australian wines.

Many more businesses than today also delivered customers' orders. This was vital as few families had their own transport. Today the sole survivor of the daily delivery, in this area at least, is the milkman. However, back in the 1920s when this photograph was taken in Petersfield, Godfrey's would be far from unusual in offering a daily bread delivery around the district. They could also supply other provisions, including 'Matchless Teas'.

This group of characters in Elstead held an enviable reputation. They were the fastest carrot diggers in the area. The villages south of Farnham are located on mainly sandy soils, which warm up quickly in the spring. This made them an ideal location for carrot growing. Note the length of some the men are holding.

Elstead, mid way between Farnham and Godalming, had a quick and good road connection to the railway station at Milford and this meant that these men could harvest their crop and have it on board a train for the London market much faster than anyone else.

These men are working with small sickles in fields at Wallington. They are harvesting lavender, a crop which today is rarely found in the county. The lavender was either used directly to ward off other smells, or sent to factories where the essential oil was extracted for use in perfumes.

Once the growth of such aromatic crops was widespread throughout

the county due to its proximity to London where there was much demand. However, it is prone to disease attack and the fields can only be used for this purpose for a while before the growing has to move elsewhere. Today the main centre of lavender production is Norfolk.

A carter heads towards Farnham Market from Crondall with a load of mangolds in 1953. He is passing the large house at Clare Park, which by this time had been converted to a private girls school in luxurious surroundings.

Rural Recollections
by Monica Jones

DEVON BULLOCKS were fattened by my grandfather during the winter months; fed large quantities of cotton and linseed cake, they provided excellent manure for the hops.

At their peak, the cattle were driven nine miles across the Hog's Back to Guildford market. This hazardous job required a sizeable posse of men, two going ahead to shut all the gates to fields and private gardens, others on either side to stop them breaking through gaps in the roadside hedge and at road junctions and several following behind. One bullock that escaped was not recaptured for two days.

The cattle were tired and sweaty when they arrived, looking far from their best and the butchers only paid £17 to £20 a head for them.

Sam Marshall, a successful Surrey farmer born in 1864, started his life as a plough boy and later he and his team took their turn carting corn to the various mills. The horses were decorated, with three

bells on the first, two on the second and one on the third. A shilling or a bundle of straw was given to the carter for beer money and often the miller would hand out a jug of the best ale.

Later, large crops of potatoes were grown, popular new varieties being The British Queen, The Giant and Up-to-Dates.

Sam Marshall also described taking hops to Wey Hill Fair, the then market for hops near Andover and the meeting-place for brewers from the west. The hop growers put up for a week there with booths at which they opened up their samples. This was also a fair for cheeses which would be bought in bulk, having travelled from the west in the waggons that returned there loaded with hops.

Wey Hill Fair was also the place to go for a good cart horse and many times hops were bartered or 'chopped over' for a colt. There was a large sheep fair where anything up to 20,000 animals were penned and winter flocks were bought. Small wonder the old mud huts which stood in for public houses and where the 'good old eighteenpenny ale' was always on sale, did brisk business.

In time, Wey Hill went out of use and the hops were sent to the new market in Borough, London. They travelled by rail and during the war, when the railways were a constant enemy target, my uncle lost track of two trucks of hops for several weeks because of the bomb destruction of the line; eventually they were found in a siding. In December 1940, 272 pockets of his hops were destroyed when Borough was bombed.

In the 1950s, as a reporter with the *Herald*, I regularly attended the fatstock shows at Farnham Market – a successor to the old-time cattle and sheep fairs held in Castle Street. Afterwards, the rosetted carcasses were seen proudly displayed in the butchers' windows around the town.

Farnham market has long since vanished to make way for Sainsbury's. It was out-lasted by Alton. I remember, in my reporting days, being invited to an evening meal by a Hampshire village vicar whom I called on regularly and who was always good for a bit of a village gossip.

He had been to Alton market (I envisaged him riding there, Friar Tuck-like, on a donkey, but I

Another load of grain arrives for the millstones at Headley Mill aboard the miller's lorry.

think that was a bit too way out) to get a goose. He was a connoisseur of antiques and the polished dining table was laid with silver candelabra and place settings and cut glass finger bowls in which violets and primroses floated.

He had a large pet Labrador dog and at mealtimes sounded an enormous brass gong, whereupon the dog bounded in to join the guests at table. It was a memorable meal, and I enjoyed every bizarre visit to that beautiful old vicarage, now a private house like so many others, along with village post offices and schools.

The Tice lorry fleet stands outside the old hop kiln at Badshot Lea in around 1938. Although hops were still grown around the building, it was also used to store the vegetables produced on the farm which the lorries carried daily to Covent Garden market in London.

S. Bide & Sons ran a large nursery business to the east of Farnham, straddling the main road to Guildford and centred on Runfold. They also grew hops and vegetables, and were renowned for their rose bushes, which were displayed in a special area just off to the right of the photograph above. To deliver their produce and plants to market and customer alike they used the lorry below, which looks very smart as it has just taken part in a 'vehicle inspection parade' according to the sign fixed to the door frame.

Chapter 8
Country Childhood

THESE three young ladies, photographed at haymaking time, epitomise the popular view of childhood in the country. It was seen as being a far more healthy upbringing than one in the town or city. True, there was certainly fresher air than in the smog-cloaked urban areas, but the life could be much harder. Children were expected to help out in the fields and at home, schools were virtually empty at harvest time and often extended the summer holiday to take account.

The playground was the whole of the locality, virtually nowhere was off limits. Doubtless there were dangers, but no more than in towns, just different. Rivers and weirs as opposed to runaway horses and carts, for instance.

Cold winter evenings were different though. Electricity came to the countryside much later than to the town. Some outlying houses in Tilford were not connected until the mid-1960s. Radios, where there were any, were powered by accumulators, collected and recharged every week. Television was unheard of.

But country children had no need of such luxuries, they learned of their world first hand. And what an upbringing it was. They became fit, tough and independent, ready to face adult life and whatever it threw at them.

Young Sid Dadson enjoys the luxury of a fireside bath in the living quarters of the post office and shop at Millbridge, Frensham at the beginning of the 20th century.

Mothers and their babies look their best for a contest at a fête in Badshot Lea during 1952. Fourth from the left in the back row is Betty Nobell (née Howard) and front right is Elaine Lunn, formerly Miss Bendal.

These two school photographs show that large classes are far from new. The infants above are engaged in handwriting practise using sand trays to save the cost of paper. Those with a tendency to be left-handed are made to keep that arm behind their back, as can be seen with the nearest girl in the back row.

Reading round the class is the order of the day for the 49 older children below, who all have their books held up at the correct angle.

Photographers used to travel around the schools, taking one form at a time, or, in small schools, the whole establishment in one shot. This still happens today, but individual portraits are taken too. Even then the photographer had to number each shot to keep track of which school was which. This particular glass plate negative was numbered '103' with a label on the front desk.

Work outside the classroom was as important as the '3Rs' in a country school. The pupils' education prepared them for a practical working life in the rural economy. Thus work in the school garden helped prepare the boys for agricultural labour.

At Hale School each pupil was given his own plot to cultivate with vegetables and here we see them hard at work to ensure their produce was the best.

A similar scene here at Badshot Lea in 1905 with Mr Edwards posing with his evening continuation class in the school garden. Mr Edwards was a professional gardener during the day and took this class in his spare time.

Badshot Lea school stands at the crossroads in the centre of the village. Here a group of pupils stand in the centre of the junction at the beginning of the 20th century, after the day's school was over. Today traffic lights control the passing vehicles and recreating this scene would be very dangerous.

A school in a different league was that alongside the village green at Tilford. This is a 'Dame' school and the teacher was Mrs Eade, who stands at her garden gate talking to a parent while her children watch the photographer. At the time school fees were 2d a week, but all Tilford House estate tenants' children were paid for by the owner's wife, Mrs Ware. Later a new, larger school was built on the other side of the green and this, although enlarged, remains in use today as All Saints School.

Joan Tice introduces Ian Goatlee to a calf at Runfold Farm in 1921.

Rural Recollections
by Monica Jones

THE COUNTRYSIDE, and above all a farm, must be the best place in the world to grow up. Life is always exciting, always changing, yet always the same. I grew up in the depression years before the war – precarious and often desperate times for farmers and farm-workers alike, yet mine was a rich and fulfilling childhood.

Although we saw little of our father and only ate with our parents on Sundays, we were lucky to enjoy the space of the farmhouse, while our friends in the village were often crammed (sometimes a family of 10) into a terraced cottage. But we suffered from chronic chilblains in a house largely unheated except for a couple of open fires, the kitchen grate and the odd paraffin stove – and in spite of our liberty bodices with the suspenders with which our thick lisle stockings were fastened. But chilblains, like fleas, were just a fact of life.

Our life was governed by the seasons, the farming year and the church calendar, all reassuringly constant. The best ingredient was the freedom, only interrupted by school, homework and church, plus a few not too arduous chores. The farm, its animals and its succession of dramas, was on our doorstep. Beyond, open to us on foot or bicycle, the fields, the woods and Crooksbury Hill.

At Whitsun, we slept in a shepherd's hut – later, in the early years of the war, I slept on top of a haystack and watched the 'Few' dog-fighting with the German planes overhead, regardless of my school certificate examinations next day. At hay-making time, we picnicked among the waist-high grasses, the sorrel and dog-daisies 'down the Moors' at the back of the house. One friend remembers riding the shire horses through the Moors to the forge at Tongham to be shod.

The start of the summer holidays meant six whole weeks of freedom, though our village friends had to go back to school before we did, and then break up again for hop-picking in September. There was never a problem about what to do. We had few outings (certainly no theme parks). Sometimes we went to Frensham Pond, or as a special treat my father drove us to Somerset Farm at Elstead in his new V8. There we ate fresh bread rolls made on an

The three Tice sisters, Betty, Monica and Joan, 'on board' a farm lorry at their Runfold home.

oil-fired stove, with thick yellow cream, strawberry jam and bananas.

Sometimes my mother took us for a week's seaside holiday, staying in a boarding house at Cliftonville or Margate (my father could never come, because of the harvest), but we really liked to be left to our own devices: scrumping apples in the orchard with our village friends, playing scrappy tennis or croquet on the lawn (we once pinned down an unwelcome visiting cousin with croquet hoops), or making scent out of rose petals.

The hay-barn was always full of kittens. Next to it was the bull's shed. A favourite 'dare' was to walk across a narrow beam from one side to the other, within feet of the angry horned and ring-nosed tossing head beneath. There were calves to feed and we had a pet

For these youngsters this is probably their first sight of farm animals in the flesh. They come from a London school and are staying at the ILEA centre at Marchant's Hill, Hindhead and are visiting Upper Ridgeway Farm at Churt in 1979. Unfortunately, today's youngsters do not have the benefit of this first-hand introduction to the countryside as Marchant's Hill was closed down in budget cuts during 1991.

lamb that grew into a fleet-footed ram, which could jump any fence to follow us down to the sweetshop in the village.

There was always something exciting happening in the farmyard, into which we could see by standing on the lavatory seat in the bathroom and looking over the fence. A favourite money-spinner was charging our friends a penny to stand on the seat for a grandstand view of the cows being brought to the bull - I don't think we had a clue what it was all about, but it was satisfyingly dramatic.

I often sat and read undisturbed in the outside (once the only) loo in a hazel copse at the bottom of the garden, full of earth smells, creepy-crawlies and leaf shadows. And I spent one whole summer holiday imagining the just-built Hog's Back Hotel rising from the distant ridge was a fairy castle, peopled by our hens, guinea-fowl, bantams and geese in the role of princes.

And then came hop-picking – a hard-working time for our friends, but for us a time of potatoes baked in the ashes of the kiln fires, and sardines and murder played in the shadowy and redolent recesses.

More young farm visitors are shown here, although some are more regular than others. Above, the children are checking out the farmer's crop of oats. The boy in the centre is playing a home made 'penny whistle', just one of many toys that could be made for nothing in the countryside.

Below young members of the Turk family pose with one of the cows on their Grovelands holding in Bentley, next to the mill.

The children from Badshot Lea Sunday School had an annual treat, usually involving a picnic. On the occasion shown they had not travelled far. They are sitting on the grassy slopes of Farnham Park, which enjoy magnificent views over the town centre.

A less formal group of Badshot Lea children this time. They have congregated in the meadow to witness the fate of an errant balloon from the Royal Balloon Factory at Farnborough in around 1913. This escaped from what later became the Royal Aircraft Establishment during testing, and drifted the intervening five miles before finally returning to 'terra firma'.

To occupy the village youths and keep them out of mischief, many communities set up boys clubs. These were basically offshoots of the working men's institutes and offered similar activities. In 1908 Baden-Powell, who lived at Pax Hill, Bentley, started the Scouting movement and this provided a nationally-based youth organisation, quickly followed by the Guides in 1910. Here a small village troop of Boy Scouts pose with their drums and bugles soon after formation.

For younger children, day nurseries were organised to look after them while their parents were at work. This is the Red Cross nursery based in the old Trimmer's Cottage Hospital, off East Street in Farnham, during 1945 or 1946.

Country children would amuse themselves playing anywhere. These youngsters are playing on the clapper bridge over the Shire Brook at Barford Ford in Churt. This lies on the county boundary between Hampshire and Surrey and the photograph was taken just before the new road bridge was built to spoil the children's fun.

Other country children had a better standard of living. This farmer's son, Alan Tice, had his own pony, Joey, and he used the animal, in 1916, for transport to Farnham Grammar School from his Runfold home.

Chapter 9

The Martial Imprint

ALL OF THE British countryside was affected by the two world conflicts of the 20th century, not least because such a large proportion of the male workforce had gone overseas to fight for king and country. However, the area covered by this book has come under the military influence for far longer, and on a continuous basis, for good and bad. The reason for this is its proximity to the two large army bases at Aldershot, the traditional 'Home of the British Army', and Bordon.

The huge numbers of troops here brought problems as well as prosperity. When off duty, and slightly the worse for drink, they could cause major problems. The worst of these occasions probably occurred during World War Two when Canadian troops ran amok in Aldershot virtually destroying the town centre in one night.

This photograph shows one of the benefits. With the building of the huge new barracks in Aldershot, the troops housed here created a prodigious amount of laundry. Some of this came to Hale Laundry, just north of Farnham. Here a well-loaded steam lorry and trailer arrives alongside the pond that gave the laundry its water supply. On the right of the small group is George Utting.

This John Henry Knight photograph probably dates from around 1880, relatively soon after Aldershot saw its major development into an army camp from a tiny village.

The photograph is taken from above Heath End and in the distance can be seen some of the massive barrack blocks stretching away toward North Camp. On the left is the garrison church and in front of it the Royal Pavilion, so beloved by Queen Victoria as a place to stay when she came to review her troops. Away to the far right, the tower of the Cambridge Military Hospital can just be made out. This is a rare survivor of these impressive buildings, despite having been closed in defence cuts some years ago.

Huge areas of land around Aldershot and Bordon were bought up or leased to provide training grounds for the newly arrived troops. Here soldiers march back to Aldershot following an exercise on Frensham Common in the 1900s. They are passing Millbridge crossroads, and a couple of locals have turned out to watch. To help the seven-mile journey pass more smoothly, the soldiers are accompanied by a military band.

This is the enormous Frensham Camp set up each year during the summer on the common between the two Frensham Ponds. In the background of this photograph taken from King's Ridge can be seen the Great Pond. The line of the camp road between the tents is roughly that occupied by the main Farnham to Hindhead road today. When the photograph was taken the public highway went around the far side of the pond, passing the Frensham Pond Hotel. All the land in the photograph now comes under the protection of the National Trust.

A Royal Horse Artillery unit is drawn up on high ground during an exercise somewhere in the area around Aldershot at about the time of World War One. The wheels of the guns and limbers can just be seen through the forest of horses' legs. They seem to be preparing for a practise charge, and one hopes the dog in the foreground moved before the bugler sounded the off.

When the situation was looking bleak during the first global conflict, the War Department asked for ideas from the civilian populace that would help the war effort. Farnham inventor John Henry Knight rose to the challenge and designed this catapult, which seems more suited to mediaeval sieges than trench warfare. It was designed to throw grenades over the full width of no man's land and was surprisingly effective.

The version shown here is the Mark II model, which is being tested on a field close to the brewery in West Street, Farnham. This field later became the Memorial Recreation Ground in memory of those who lost their lives in the war.

The War Department declined to put the device into use, but amazingly both versions still survive. The Mark I is in the Museum of Farnham and the Rural Life Centre houses the version shown here.

Young Ted Porter, the right-hand soldier home on leave with a friend during 1907, visits his family in Tice's hop ground at Badshot Lea, where they were busy picking that season's crop. Left to right are Cis Porter, Sid Monk, Ern Porter, Dolly Porter, Alf Porter and their mother.

This soldier has arrived home in King's Road, Aldershot in time to wave his family and other residents off on a charabanc outing to the seaside. There are over 20 passengers in this three horse-drawn vehicle.

With the disappearance of most of the male workforce to fight in the trenches during World War One, women were drafted in to help sow, tend and harvest the crops that were equally vital to the survival of the British nation.

Here four Land Army members are working with a harrow on Runfold Farm in 1919. They are being instructed by a male companion, and even a year after the war's end the women's help was still much needed as so many men were lost during the conflict.

These World War One Land Army girls are taking part in a parade at Rowledge, probably to raise funds for the welfare of troops overseas. Unfortunately the rest of the wording on the banner is unreadable.

After the war most of the women returned to more traditional occupations. However, a similar need arose during World War Two and again the nation's women came forward in vast numbers. This time they were organised in a more formal Women's Land Army, which looked after their welfare as well as allocating work.

Women's Land Army girls pose on the bonnet of a Surrey War Agricultural Executive Committee lorry, which will shortly take them home from the day's work somewhere in the Farnham area during World War Two.

Rural Recollections
by Monica Jones

DUNG from the nearby army barracks was spread on the fields of our farm. Before World War One, the cavalry, the Royal Horse Artillery and the Royal Field Artillery were stationed in Aldershot and my father had a contract with the army to keep the pits at the stables clear of manure.

Each morning during the winter, three teams (waggons drawn by two horses apiece) would set out at five for the cavalry barracks. On their way back, the carters stopped for a pint of beer halfway (the pubs opened at six in the morning then); fortunately, the horses knew their way home.

When war broke out, the best horses were requisitioned for army use on payment of £60 a head. One or two were saved from the eagle eye of the inspecting officer by taking off their shoes and

turning them out to grass; he assumed they were lame. After the war, the government loaned out the army horses to work on the farm; two black heavy artillery horses made a fine team.

The army was always there, adding spice to our rural routine. On the sultry June nights of my childhood, the Aldershot Military Tattoo added to the flashes and crashes of the thunderstorms, with their ever-present threat of blight hanging over the hops.

Two poplars stood by the old wall bounding the front lawn of the farmhouse; in years past, they had guided visiting waggons crossing the Hog's Back down to the farm. Beneath them was a stone pillar at the entrance to the drive and on this we sat as children to wave to the troops, in lorries or foot-slogging, as they passed along our narrow lane cross-country to manoeuvres at Frensham and Hankley.

Many of the girls were trained in unfamiliar skills. Among the more unusual was thatching and here a team are at work thatching ricks of harvested corn on Heath Farm, Munstead, Godalming. Besides ricks they were also called upon to repair the roofs of farm buildings from time to time.

rolled on top and dungarees daringly nipped in at the waist. Later in the war, German prisoners of war were drafted in, living in farm cottages, and some stayed on afterwards, marrying local girls. German submarine crews, sent from a camp at Guildford to pick hops, objected to muddying their boots in the hop gardens.

Every possible bit of land was cultivated for the war effort – copses and commons, parks and golf courses. Eyes were cast at Frensham Pond, drained to avoid it being used as a landmark for bombers. It was discarded as being too boggy after my uncle, who was chairman of the Surrey War Agricultural Committee, sank into the mud to prove the point. Sweetcorn was grown on the farm for the first time to feed Canadian and American troops.

Two incidents brought the war closer to home. A neighbouring farm was reduced to rubble by a flying bomb or doodle bug; the farmer's wife was killed, cows were blown into the trees, and the surviving animals were given temporary shelter at our farm. An ammunition train parked on a nearby disused railway line was bombed, providing a spectacular firework display; a shed in which a

Later, the woods which crowded the hill once topped by an ancient earthwork known as Soldiers' Ring, sheltered bivouacked and net-shrouded lorries of World War Two New Zealand troops quartered in the big houses, and camouflaged vehicles were ranked along the Hog's Back in the run-up to D-Day.

In the early days of the war, in September 1939, the air raid sirens of the 'phoney war' caused some alarm, soon to be replaced by cheerful sang-froid. Later, townsfolk were only too glad to spend their holidays helping on the farms under the slogan 'Back to the Land'. An added incentive was the extra rations of tea, margarine, cheese and sugar, which were also doled out in their ounces weekly to the queue of eager hop-pickers.

Farm-workers became fewer and fewer as the men went off to war and the Women's Land Army arrived. Twenty years earlier my mother had met my father as a World War One London-born land girl working on the farm.

As teenagers, we were deeply jealous of Sheila, the land girl billeted with us, with her long blonde hair

Many areas of recreational land were dug up to increase food production during both world wars. These girls are sowing potatoes in Farnham Park, a large area of open land north of the town now used by walkers and as grazing for small numbers of cattle.

farmworker and his family sheltered grew red hot as burning debris showered onto the corrugated iron roof and two men were awarded the George Cross for their bravery in uncoupling the trucks.

The war ended our country childhood; midway through it, we were gone, my elder sister into the WRNS, my younger as a naval VAD. I joined the ATS, manning the ack-ack guns and driving ambulances at Dover. After the war, tractors took over from horses and steam-driven threshers, machines replaced the hop-pickers who now had money to spend on less arduous holidays; sand and gravel digging swallowed up the hay meadows and cornfields and in the end a multi-lane highway cut a swathe across the country lane within feet of the farm.

The local area has always been used to a strong military presence in its midst regardless of whether the country was at war or otherwise. Above, General French and the Prince of Teck stand in the middle of Badshot Lea village crossroads, as a column of troops 'on manoeuvres' pauses for a break in 1904. Less than 40 years later the means of transport had changed dramatically, shown below by a column of Cruiser Mark IV tanks passing through Thursley village during an exercise on the surrounding commons, before leaving for North Africa. The building in the background is the old vicarage, which is also shown, in earlier times, in the Home Life chapter.

During World War Two uniforms were in evidence everywhere, both on and off duty.

The group of despatch riders above are members of the Seale and Sands Home Guard. 'Dads' Army' units were established everywhere and when the call went out for volunteers to join, vast numbers came forward from the rural workforce to forego their limited leisure hours for the good of the country.

Below, a mixed group of servicemen and Home Guards pose outside their 'local', the Cricketers at Hale, during a period of leave. Among them are soldiers, airmen and Air Raid Precautions personnel.

These two highly-detailed photographs recall the peace celebrations in Overton, near Andover in Hampshire, during June 1902. On 31 May the signing of the Treaty of Vereeniging brought an end to the Boer War. This conflict had begun in October 1899 and large numbers of British troops had been drafted to South Africa, many never to return. All the villagers had turned out to witness the passing parade, including the school children who had earlier formed up in costume in the school playground.

Following World War One and its vast numbers of casualties, the British public raised funds to provide war memorials for virtually every village and town in the country. Within a couple of years most of these had been erected and dedicated and they became the focus for remembrance parades which continue right up to the present day.

Above, the residents of Wrecclesham turned out in large numbers for the dedication of their memorial on the edge of the cemetery opposite the parish church. A similar occasion is recorded below as wreaths are laid at Seale where the memorial stands right beside the road.

Following World War Two, celebrations were held throughout the country, first on VE Day, which marked the end of the war in Europe, and later when Japan surrendered following the dropping of the atomic bomb. Here Mike Stenning rings the school bell at Churt to mark the start of the village's celebrations of the former event.

The military influence went very deep and had effects beyond the more obvious. Here Tilford Fife and Drum Band pose for their photograph outside the village institute in 1911. Their uniform owes much to the style of the troops that passed by on their way to exercise on the nearby commons. The band is now long gone, but their drum is on display at the Rural Life Centre alongside their history, helping recall the martial imprint.

Chapter 10

On The Move

THE PACE of life in the country has always seemed slower and more relaxed than that of the town. This is reflected in all aspects, not least in the means of transport in use at any particular time.

Road standards, if you can call them roads, lagged way behind. The lanes were often no more than muddy, rutted tracks with little or no metalling to speak of. Tarmac came much later and even then the roads still retained their narrow proportions. It is said that the deeper a byway is sunken into its surroundings, the older it is. If this is the case, then many local roads must be very ancient indeed.

The type of transport in use was dictated by the terrain which it had to cross. Hence these loads of woolsacks bound for market in the Cranleigh area need a lot of motive power to carry them over the heavy clay soils of the district. Each waggon has eight oxen in harness and the wheels have wide rims, fitted with strakes, to prevent them sinking into the mud.

The coming of first canals and then the railways increased the speed with which the farmers could get their produce to market. Road improvements allowed the passage of motorised vehicles too, but also opened up the countryside to visitors on bicycles and motor cycles and in cars and coaches. All this led to increased prosperity for the country dwellers and the discovery of untapped markets.

A covered waggon and team of four plods up the steep Gravel Hill from the Bourne towards Farnham in the early years of the 20th century. The road is, as yet, unmade, but drainage has been put in.

Rural Recollections
by Monica Jones

HORSES, from Shetland ponies to feather-fetlocked shires, were an intrinsic but always enchanting part of my pre-war country childhood. On the farm, we had a team of eight matched dapple greys, collected over many years of painstaking visits to horse sales. Captain, Major, Duke and their team-mates were as hard-working as any other of the farm horses, but as their names imply, they had added presence and glamour, even on an ordinary working day out ploughing or pulling one of the Sturt waggons, piled high at hop-picking time.

But it was at the ploughing matches and agricultural shows that they came into their own, winning many cash prizes and silver cups. We children would lie in the hay-loft over the stables, peering down through the trap-door as the carters worked by hurricane lamplight in the early morning over their magnificent charges who stood patiently, proudly conscious of the fuss. Their dapple coats were groomed until they shone, their white 'socks' and tails washed and brushed, their manes plaited and braided with scarlet, yellow and royal blue ribbons, their ears enclosed in ear-caps decorated with bright-coloured bobbles and their hooves varnished. The leather and brasses of their harness were polished to high brilliance.

The horses drank from a stone water-trough in the yard outside, the chaff from their lips feeding the ancient goldfish there – I never worked out how the fish avoided a watery path down the horses' gullets.

We often rode on the horses or the waggons, but my first experience of four-footed transport was a donkey, Billy, and donkey-cart I was given on my third birthday. Billy was obstinate and cantankerous, given to pulling off his rider's shoe and eating it or chasing a would-be captor and nipping her exposed behind as she fled either over or under the five-barred gate. There were always ponies about and the Shetland, misnamed Merrylegs, was as bad-tempered as Billy, dragging my six-year-old sister across country with her foot caught in the stirrup.

As a 12-year-old schoolboy, my uncle rode his pony Joey to Farnham Grammar School and often less than reluctantly missed the last lesson when Joey escaped from his shed and had to be removed from illicit grazing on the cricket pitch.

Superseded by lorries, tractors and cars, few horses remained on the farms after World War Two. In the following years, when I was a reporter on the *Farnham Herald*, we would crowd into the office windows to watch the horse-drawn gipsy caravans passing through the town along West Street en route for the Bentley and Alton hop grounds. The Hen and Chicken pub, at Upper Froyle on the A31, was the setting in past years for the annual gipsy horse fair.

Churches in the villages round about were often the scenes of mass christenings and even multiple

A fully loaded hop waggon pauses before setting off for market from Tice's Runfold Farm in 1919. One horse was all that was needed for this enormous though relatively light load, which also included some hay for food on the journey.

weddings at hop-picking time. I attended one gipsy king's funeral and watched the ceremonial burning of his caravan.

In more recent years, the magnificent trotters raced by some of the caravan dwellers have shown off their paces around town and countryside (at one time they raced along the Hog's Back until this was barred) and stirred blood first stirred 70 years ago by those gracious dapple greys.

Gipsy hop pickers, complete with their homes and chattels, pass along Crondall Lane in Farnham during September 1956 after another successful harvest in the Farnham, Bentley and Alton gardens.

Once the hops had been successfully used in the brewing of beer, the end product needed to be got back to the rural workforce for consumption after a hard and dusty day spent in the fields.

Two brewer's drays in these photographs contrast the change from horse to petrol power. Above the Courage & Barclay's horse-drawn variety is just about to pull away from the Queen's Hotel at Selborne, very near to Alton where the cargo was made. A chain-driven Thornycroft lorry was probably a recent acquisition of Farnham United Breweries in 1913 when this photograph is thought to have been taken. The vehicle is outside the Fox public house in the Bourne and the driver is Frederick Goolding. His mate was probably Mr E. Challis.

Here, high on the Hogs Back between Farnham and Guildford, the Victory Inn made an attractive destination for a weekend walk or ride for locals and visitors alike. It enjoyed superb views over the local countryside in all directions. Unfortunately it was demolished during a road improvement scheme many years ago.

A similar fate befell the Happy Home *(below)*, which was located in the Bourne, right opposite the Fox featured earlier. The two pubs created a bottleneck on the main road from Farnham to Hindhead and one of them had to go in 1956 to make the road safer for passing traffic.

Improving road surfaces led to ever increasing speeds and the inevitable road accident had to happen sooner or later. This sad occasion at Hook, near Odiham in Hampshire, proved fatal for at least one of the occupants in February 1914. The junction here is still an accident black spot today, where a local road crosses the main highway from London to Basingstoke and the west.

With the coming of the motor vehicle, the days of the village blacksmith's horse-shoeing activities were numbered. Many realised the implications and the earliest garages sprang up around the forges.

Wheelwrights and carriage builders began to make motor bodies, as here in West Street, Farnham, where wooden-framed coachwork is being built on to bought-in chassis. However, it was not to be long before the factory-made car put paid to these small scale enterprises.

Road building and repair provided another avenue of work for country dwellers. Here men are at work cutting a new road by Smugglers' Way in the Sands, just outside Farnham. They have felled the obstructing trees and are now about to set to work on the road surface itself.

This gang of roadmen pose for the photographer outside the parish church at Badshot Lea. They are hand-tarring the road to Runfold for the first time in its history. Atop the boiler for heating the tar is Jack North.

This steam road locomotive *(left)* belonged to Sellson-Willson & Co. of Dartford, Kent, who were contractors. It has probably come to Hetherington's iron works at Alton for repairs while employed locally.

The Wey Iron Works produced much agricultural equipment, some of their own patent design, including flooring for hop kilns which could be rolled back to retrieve the dried crop.

A threshing gang pause for a break in one of the many public houses in Alton High Street. The wooden threshing machine, or 'drum', is well sheeted up to protect it from the weather. Such contractors' gangs were a common sight on country roads in the autumn as they travelled from farm to farm.

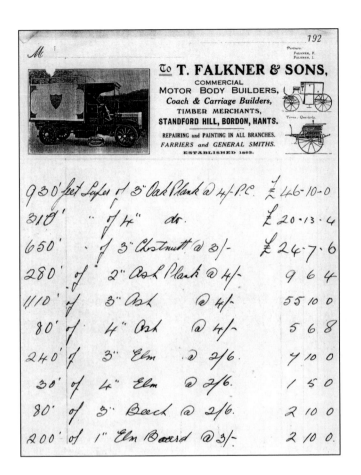

This timber order was issued by Falkner's coach building works in Standford Hill, Bordon in the 1920s. It illustrates an interesting period when horse-drawn vehicles were still being produced alongside their motorised equivalents.

This Vulcan motor lorry of the Junior Army & Navy Stores at Aldershot is ready to set off with driver Jack Peal, right, to deliver goods to the surrounding district. Perhaps country dwellers did not find shopping so easy years ago, especially for larger items, but the stores seemed far more obliging with their delivery services to outlying settlements.

The canal age brought limited benefits to the area covered by this book. Unlike the industrial heartland of the country where heavy loads could be more easily moved, this area, with its undulating countryside and more easily portable finished products, did not offer the same benefits.

Despite this, the River Wey from Weybridge south to Guildford was the first to be canalised in Britain. The Wey Navigation offered a convenient route to the large London market and this photograph by John Henry Knight shows a lock on the waterway, thought to be at Ripley.

Later the canal was extended to Godalming to meet with the Wey and Arun Canal to give a through route from London to the south coast. The latter was not successful, arriving too late to compete with the expanding railways. The second photograph shows the steam tug *Jumna* at Littlehampton, heading for the southern entrance to the canal at Arundel with a sailing barge in tow.

Nearby water could be a blessing and a curse. Above, the River Wey flows beneath Eashing Bridge near Godalming, providing an attractive setting for these cottages.

The photograph below shows the result of the melting of heavy winter snows during the 1920s at Bentworth near Alton. The lorry is struggling to get through the flood from the village pond caused by the rapid thaw. To the right, boards have been laid to provide a makeshift walkway for pedestrians.

Before it gets to Eashing, the River Wey flows alongside the Farnham to Godalming road at Elstead. This stretch is always prone to flooding and here a Dennis Lancet III bus belonging to the Aldershot & District Traction Co. struggles through the inundation in 1950 or 1951.

Besides the Aldershot & District services, local villages were also served by the Yellow Bus Services' fleet, seen here at the company's Guildford base along with their crews.

The coming of the railways in the late 18th century heralded a dramatic improvement in longer distance transport, particularly 'up to London'. This is Witley station, south of Godalming on the Guildford to Portsmouth line, fairly soon after opening in 1875. What is not seen in this view is the very deep cutting at the end of which the station lies.

The railways brought more employment for the rural population. Because the stations were generally only located in larger towns, there was a need for transport for travellers to outlying settlements and farms. Fly proprietors sprang up to operate an embryo taxi service, based near to each station. Here some of the Haslemere vehicles and drivers are lined up outside the Railway Hotel, directly opposite the town's station.

Fire brigades began as bands of volunteers recruited by the insurance companies to fight town fires with manually propelled and pumped appliances. Horse power allowed them to cover a wider area and steam pumps helped in the tackling of larger fires.

Here the Haslemere brigade are just about to leave Shottermill Ponds after filling the tank of their steam-powered appliance. The fire engine still exists, preserved in a museum at Cobh in the Republic of Ireland.

You can never be sure what you are going to meet around the next corner on a country road. Probably one of the most unusual sights must have been these elephants, seen just after leaving their train at Farnham station. They were bound for a circus tour of the district in September 1952.

Chapter 11

Festivals and Folklore

COUNTRY FOLK have celebrated the passing of the seasons and the bounty it brings since time immemorial. The tradition continues today, but added to it have been national and international events such as the ending of wars and coronations or jubilees.

The manner of the celebrations may have been simpler than in towns and cities, but they were still very much anticipated and enjoyed. Like much larger settlements, Badshot Lea was no exception in holding its own annual carnival through the village streets. The villagers did not have lorries to transport the revellers through the village in 1951,

they had the farm waggons from Tice's farm. Back in the dim and distant past, unexpected happenings were explained by the invention of legends concerning gods and mystical beings. This tradition has continued, with the legends and more recent happenings becoming the stuff of local folklore.

Again such events are celebrated in the villages concerned, often in a unique way. Sometimes, though, the folklore reaches the printed page, albeit somewhat embellished, and survives as a strange mix of fiction and fact which today becomes subject matter for contemporary artforms.

May heralded the start of summer and the end of the long dark winter with its short days. Crops began to grow and the land was full of promise. To celebrate, country communities have always observed May Day at or near the beginning of the month. Maypoles were erected on many a village green and the school children performed their intricate dances.

However, in some places like Blackmoor near Bordon the celebration took another form. Here the children, including three sisters at the front of this group, carried their May garland from house to house in 1902, collecting pennies or sweets and ushering in the better weather and longer days.

Toward the other end of the month, the residents of Rowledge traditionally hold their annual fête and sports. The latter involves many novelty races, such as wheelbarrow and egg and spoon, and even the more serious ones are not just for the children. This is the mothers' race in full flight during one such event in the early 1960s.

Traditionally around the winter solstice, mummers plays, each with its own slight variation, were performed in many villages. The tale is a strange mixture of religion, the stories of death and resurrection, and St George and the dragon. Many of the village stories were thought to be lost forever, but research has recovered enough details to allow their revival where landlords are prepared to allow the players to perform on Boxing Day. Here Crookham Mummers perform outside the Chequers public house in their home village on a particularly fine December day, thought to be in 1978.

Some villages put on their own versions of much larger celebrations. Badshot Lea erected this miniature 'Skylon' reflecting the full size version in London for 1951's Festival of Britain exhibition. It was constructed in the corner of the churchyard closest to the village crossroads with the blessing of the Revd Roberts, in the centre of the group, the village's priest in charge.

Fresh from its berth in Badshot Lea Docks (a small pond that periodically flooded the village's main street) the *Saucy Kipper* made its first appearance in the Aldershot Hospital carnival during 1904. The float won first prize, and henceforth the village football team were known as the 'Dockers'.

Rural Recollections
by Monica Jones

COUNTRY FESTIVALS were mostly linked to the church calendar, giving a reassuring sense of continuity.

First came Plough Sunday in January, with a special service to 'Speed the plough'. I don't remember that we ever made much of Valentine's Day – except to look for the birds beginning to nest – though I do have a Valentine card sent by my grandfather to my grandmother when they were courting in 1876. Lace-edged, it pictures a steaming kettle and the daring inscription 'Our steam is up and my love is at boiling point' – but it was some years before they were married.

March came in like the proverbial lion with St David's Day. Leeks grown on the farm were meticulously cleaned and trimmed. They went to the Welch Guards in Aldershot to be paraded in the military caps behind the band and white goat mascot.

Mid-way through Lent, with chocolate virtuously given up for six whole weeks, came Mothering Sunday. For us 1930s children, this was not Mother's Day demanding a rare visit to the town for an expensive card and gift.

Mothering Sunday was a day of thanksgiving for Mother Church and historically a day when servant girls returned from their 'places' in the big houses to see their own mothers, taking with them simnel cake rich with fruit and spices and marzipan, and flowers they had picked along the way. For us, there was a Sunday School expedition to the woods for the primroses and violets – a violation that wouldn't be acceptable today. In church on Mothering Sunday we presented our posies to our mothers with a self-conscious 'Thank you for all you have done' and a proffered kiss.

My memories of 1 April are dire. We invariably had boiled eggs for breakfast; there were plenty of

Monica Jones, then Miss Tice, as the family's own May Queen at her birthday party on 1 May 1932.

hens wandering about, and guinea fowl that roosted in the trees and shouted 'Come back, come back' at all and sundry. Duck eggs, collected round the pond where we played ducks and drakes, skimming flat stones over the murky water, were too strong for me, though my sister liked them.

Our breakfast eggs were relieved only after a rabbit shoot when fried rabbit legs were a yummy alternative. I was heartily sick of boiled eggs and my heart leapt when a dish with the massive silver cover usually reserved for goose or turkey was placed on the table one morning. We waited expectantly; the cover was lifted with a flourish and underneath were ranged the breakfast eggs. A tearful April Fool I certainly was.

Hot cross buns were a once-a-year Good Friday treat, made at the bakery next door. In the blessedly quiet town, the shops were closed except for the bakeries and fish shops. Potatoes were traditionally planted in gardens and allotments.

Easter Sunday found us in church again, wearing our obligatory new clothes and adding our enthusiastic 'alleluyas'. We returned home to roast chicken and our chocolate Easter eggs; I remember lying in the hayloft to relish them in solitude, but best of all was to melt them in front of the kitchen range until the chocolate dripped, to be caught on our eager tongues.

May Day was very special to me. Not only was it the first true day of summer, when following the old maxim that 'it's dabbling

Another annual celebration in most schools, either town or country, was Empire Day on 24 May. Here Badshot Lea School children parade in around 1913.

in the dew that makes the milkmaids fair' we rushed out into the early morning to scoop the dew onto our hopeful faces, but it was also my birthday.

Most villages and schools had a maypole. We had our own and I was the undisputed May Queen, year after year. The maypole with its multi-coloured streamers was set up on the lawn. I had a throne (a high-backed chair swathed with crêpe paper and ribbon). When I grew older, I wore a nip-waisted dress worn by my aunt to Edwardian dances 30 years before, gloriously spangled with gold bugle beads. My sisters and friends were my courtiers in appropriately splendid costumes from our dressing-up box.

Of course, I had a crown of flowers, and all the young guests brought posies of flowers instead of presents; afterwards we performed our intricate pattern-weaving maypole dances to music from our wind-up gramophone. And it was always sunny.

As children we followed the old country customs: we ate 'bread and cheese' – the so-called new green hedgerow shoots – listened to the yellow-hammer

Parades and street parties were organised to mark important events. Here the people of Badshot Lea turn out and hang up the bunting, probably to mark the end of the Boer War in June 1902. This is the village's main road, and the buildings are virtually unchanged today, though to hold this sort of celebration again many parked cars would have to be removed.

Below the villagers of Selborne process along the main street on their way to the parish church at the Plestor, to mark a similar occasion.

complain 'A little bit of bread and NO cheese', smoked acorn cup pipes; we sucked honey from the periwinkle and honeysuckle flowers but avoided the poisonous lords and ladies and deadly nightshade like the plague. We rubbed dock leaves on our nettle stings and made dolls out of poppies.

My father predicted: 'The oak before the ash, we're in for a splash; the ash before the oak we're in for a soak', and watched the sky anxiously on St Swithin's Day in July.

Rogation Sunday, with a procession to bless the crops, came before Ascension Day (half a day off school). At Whitsun, we camped out in the old wheeled corrugated-iron shepherd's hut.

Harvest was a time of special celebration. The crops were susceptible to the weather, so thanks were offered to gods, both Christian and heathen, for a successful year.

Above hop pickers at Puttenham have dressed in their best clothes for the last day of the picking in 1910. They pose here with some of the equipment they would have used, including one of the pockets of dried hops. The celebration of the day was all the more important because it was also pay day for the hard work that had gone before.

Again, best clothes are to the fore below with this wonderfully decorated harvest home waggon. Unfortunately the location and date are unknown but it would undoubtedly have taken part in a carnival to celebrate the end of a successful growing season.

Later came harvest festival – once, my father urged me to shout out 'No more poles' (the traditional cry to end picking) in the hop-filled church.

Christmas was the grand finale. We made expeditions to the woods for holly and ivy to twine round the polished banister down which we so joyously slid on less prickly occasions. The ceiling-high Christmas tree had real candles in little tin holders, and we ate pickled walnuts from the tree in the yard with our cold turkey and York ham at our extended family supper.

We played Up Jenkins and charades and sardines – and of course, sang carols round the piano.

These interior and exterior photographs of the Red Lion, on the old London Road at Thursley, recall a gruesome event. It was here in 1786 that an unknown sailor, on his way back to his ship at Portsmouth, fell in with three strangers who subsequently robbed and murdered him in the nearby Devil's Punchbowl.

The three, Marshal, Casey and Lonagon, were apprehended, tried and hanged. Their bodies were then left, suspended in iron cages, as a warning to others on the gibbet at Hindhead, clearly visible from the road where the deed had taken place.

Today the Red Lion is a private house and the road bypasses the murder spot, but the story is kept alive by a novel, *The Broomsquire*, written by Sabine Baring-Gould. This has recently been dramatised and is regularly performed by a travelling theatre group in halls around the area featured in the tale.

Chapter 12
Characters

T HE CHARACTERS make the countryside. Not for them the hurried, lemming-like rush each day to and from work in offices full of serried ranks of similar desks, or behind identical machines on factory floors. Everyone in the country does his or her job in their own particular, unique way.

Through the ages some of these characters have gone down in local history or folklore, but many are still alive and one place that some come together each year is at the Rural Life Centre's Rustic Sunday.

This annual celebration of country life is held at the end of July each year and brings together professional and amateur craftsmen to preserve the rural traditions.

George Nash, above, lives in Boundstone and learnt, many years ago, the traditional gipsy craft of peg making. Here he demonstrates the craft one Rustic Sunday using wooden rods split with a sharp knife, and bound together with strips cut from old tin cans.

Gipsy families old and new are represented here. Above, Betsy Ray peels potatoes at Longmoor army camp, near Bordon, to feed the troops. Born Elizabeth Mitchell around 1867, she married Jim Ray in 1887 and they lived at Barley Mow Hill, Headley.

Jim Ray was a strawberry grower and hawker, but the large Ray family boasted itinerant chimney sweeps, hawkers, basket makers, farm labourers, horse dealers and market gardeners and could trace its ancestry back to true Romany descent.

Below, in Borelli Walk, Farnham, this 'family' took up temporary residence during the 1980s. These modern-day travellers moved from temporary job to temporary job across the south of England each year from their Bristol base. Their accommodation consisted of the bow top caravan and bender tents.

Brian, on the right, made the caravans as they travelled, then sold them to raise money. Unfortunately, the money he made did not allow him to keep one in which to live permanently.

Rural Recollections
by Monica Jones

CYCLING round the Hampshire country-side, news-gathering for the *Herald* in the 1950s, I got to know two men who personified for me the richness and robustness of village life.

George Clements was the father of Binsted: chairman of the parish council, churchwarden, head of a family building business. He knew everything that went on in the village and imparted his information with relish and humour.

He always welcomed me with true country hospitality, even at dinner-time. Sometimes I found him re-soling his own or his sons' boots, in which he took great pride.

George kept bees, and on one visit pressed on me his just-broached home-made mead. On a hot day, it was cold, dry and delicious. I had a couple of glasses as I listened to the news of the village. The wine would have no effect, George assured me, and I believed him, until I got up to go and my legs buckled under me. I had to walk round the village until I felt safe enough to cycle back to the office.

Anyone – and that means everyone in Crondall – who knew Albie Ralph, will know what an extraordinary man he was: awkward certainly, often fiercely argumentative at the drop of a hat, soft-hearted and generous always.

Elected a member of Crondall Parish Council in

Emmie Langridge poses with one of the family's cows on the 30-acre smallholding at Semaphore Farm in Telegraph Lane, Four Marks, west of Alton.

George Mayes was the last of the Hindhead broomsquires, or besom makers. Here he stands outside the Broomsquire's Cottage in the bottom of the Punchbowl. This was also known as Highcombe Farm and was completely destroyed by Canadian troops during World War Two.

Harry Nixon gets a trim at this outdoor barber's shop in The Bourne, Farnham. Meanwhile a satisfied customer with a short back and sides chats to the unidentified barber.

1949, he served under the Labour banner for 30 years at a time when party politics were virtually unknown at that level of local government. His concern about what went on in council meetings never left him, even when well into his 90s.

Albie was a man of unrelenting independence and integrity. Everything was either black or white to him. It was either right for Crondall or it was wrong, and if it was wrong there was no way Albie was going to allow it an easy passage.

I first met Albie 50 years ago in the hut in the centre of the village in which he carried on his trade as the village cobbler. He had started in business on his own in 1923 at the age of 19. Most of his customers then were farm labourers, and he told me they would bring their boots to him at night for

repair by the morning because they were the only boots they had.

That hut was the true village parliament. The postman, the milkman, the sweep and many others crammed into its tiny space to discuss local issues. As the nails were hammered into the leather soles of Crondall's boots and shoes, the problems of the village were hammered out. Crondall was Albie's entire life; he boasted that he had never been farther abroad than the Isle of Wight and seldom went as far as Farnham.

It was Albie's Dickensian upbringing as well as his nature that made him such a combative Labour supporter and uncompromising champion of the under-dog. When his father died and his mother was unable to support the family, he was sent with his brothers and sister to Wimble Hill, the bleak Poor Law school for orphaned children on an exposed ridge of the Hampshire countryside. There he met Dorothy, his wife for more than 60 years.

Life was unbelievably harsh for those destitute children, who worked from the time they woke up at 6.30am until they went to bed. They had to scrub and clean the dormitory and polish the floors and make the beds before they went to school, the boys walking in procession the two miles to Farnham. They picked up chestnuts on the way to eat at school, for which they were punished if caught.

School holidays were even worse because there was no respite from work, the boys in the garden and the girls in the kitchen and laundry. Beatings were frequent, the girls with a slipper and the boys with a wooden fencing cane. Albie was always in trouble because he was outspoken and 'got stuck in' if he was angered by a particular injustice.

Things were not much better when he left Wimble Hill for a three-year apprenticeship with a boot repairer in a Surrey village. He once told me: 'He kept me ground down and when I left I made up my mind I would never let anyone do that to me again, and I never have.'

William and Frank Newell at Badshot Farm where they both worked for the tenant, Humphrey Gardener, in around 1910. When Mr Gardener retired from farming and moved to Mavins Road, Farnham, William continued to work for him as gardener despite living three miles away in The Sands.

Three local girls who joined the World War One Land Army. Muriel Middleton *(right)*, Doris Luke and Elspeth Little worked on a farm near Huntingdon in Cambridgeshire during 1918, where this photograph was taken.

Jim Lickfold demonstrates the Swiss tree bicycle at the Rural Life Centre in 1980. Jim spent much of his working life as a forester at Tilhill Forestry in Tilford, where he used the bicycle to get seed samples from the topmost branches of tall pine trees. Although retired, Jim still looks after the many and varied species in the centre's arboretum.

Daniel Rampton was born in Froyle near Alton in 1833. He fought in the Crimean War, winning two medals, before returning home to work for the family of J. Alfred Eggar as a shepherd in Bentley and Froyle. Among his 12 children was his son Fred, seen with him here. Fred joined the Navy as a boy and became a CPO before being killed in the Baltic in July 1919.

Some characters never retired. Bill Barnett was 90 when this photograph was taken in March 1959. Despite his great age he was still working as a gardener to Mrs Rome.

Mrs Martin and her sister were well-known in Elstead during the early 1950s. The Post Office was on the village green and here post mistress Mrs Martin tends one of the stamp machines attached to the posting box outside, watched by her sister off on an errand with her faithful cycle.

The merits of the local potatoes are discussed by Frank Sawkins in 1951 as he pauses from the task of lifting the crop with his trusty team. The listeners are two girls from the Elstead VA camp, who have the job of picking up the lifted tubers.

We must not overlook the myriad unnamed characters that have given the countryside its unique flavour and ensured its survival for present and future generations to enjoy.

In tribute are these two unidentified subjects who epitomise two aspects of the rural scene: agriculture and domestic service.

Despite her age of 76 in 1920, the woman *(left)* was ready for the off, complete with carpet bag, umbrella and cleanly starched apron, wherever her employer wished her to go.

Towards the end of another arduous day, the last horse team on Stovolds Cross Farm at Shackleford traces out yet another furrow under the ever watchful eye of the lonely plodding ploughman.

Index